WITH HIM

WITH HIM

Listening to the Underside of the World

BRUNO CADORÉ

Edited by Steve Cox

BLOOMSBURY CONTINUUM
LONDON · OXFORD · NEW YORK · NEW DELHI · SYDNEY

BLOOMSBURY CONTINUUM
Bloomsbury Publishing Plc
50 Bedford Square, London, WC1B 3DP, UK

BLOOMSBURY, BLOOMSBURY CONTINUUM and the Diana logo are
trademarks of Bloomsbury Publishing Plc

First published in 2018 in France as *Avec Lui, Écouter L'envers
Du Monde* by Les Éditions du Cerf
First published in Great Britain 2019

A catalogue record for this book is available from the British Library

Library of Congress Cataloguing-in-Publication data has been applied for

ISBN: PB: 978-1-4729-7015-2; ePDF: 978-1-4729-7018-3;
ePUB: 978-1-4729-7017-6

2 4 6 8 10 9 7 5 3 1

Typeset by Deanta Global Publishing Services, Chennai, India
Printed and bound in Great Britain by CPI Group (UK) Ltd, Croydon CR0 4YY

MIX
Paper from
responsible sources
FSC® C020471

To find out more about our authors and books visit www.bloomsbury.com
and sign up for our newsletters

CONTENTS

*Foreword by Timothy Radcliffe OP, Former
Master of the Dominican Order*   vii

Prologue   1

1 Becoming a Dominican   3

2 Being a Preacher   37

3 Living the Order   61

4 Encountering the World   113

5 Unfolding the Mystery   179

Epilogue   208

FOREWORD

Bruno Cadoré OP has just finished his term as Master of the Order of Preachers. The word 'Master' might suggest a bossy role, commanding obedience and imposing one's will, but this was never the case with Saint Dominic, our first Master, nor with Bruno. We are not an army but a community of brothers and sisters. Hence the name of the male Dominican religious, 'friars', *fratres*, brethren. The Master cares for our fraternity.

This spirituality of brotherhood and sisterhood – the sisters were first – was vastly attractive in the emerging urban culture of the thirteenth century when the Order was founded, with its new towns and universities, filled with strangers come from far away to trade or just out of curiosity. The vertical hierarchies of the old feudal world were weakening, and people were adapting to more horizontal relationships. Democracy was in the air. Marie-Dominique Chenu OP, one of the 'fathers' of the second Vatican Council, claimed that the word *frater* evoked the earliest days of Christianity, when 'brother' and 'sister' were the only Christian titles that counted. He claimed that for Dominic's contemporaries, they carried 'a utopian charge'.

Our society has urgent need of this spirituality of fraternity today. We are ever more mobile, in constant communication with strangers. Never has there been so much movement. This sparks fear of the stranger, and the rise of populism. The old markers of identity given by social class, religion, gender, locality and family are shaken. Our politics and personal relationships are becoming expressive of a search for identity. In this uncertain, fluid world, we need a spirituality of friendship, so that the stranger may be seen as our brother or sister.

This is also an urgent need in our Church which is living through its worst crisis since the Reformation. Indeed it *is* the crisis of the Church which came into existence in response to the Reformation. The Council of Trent gave us a new vision of priesthood, new seminaries, with a new vision of holiness. This was a vast success and it saved the Church from collapse. But it had its dangers, above all a poisonous kind of clericalism. Priests came to form an elite which was unaccountable to anyone. The full dignity of the laity was not recognized. They were there, we say, to pray, pay and obey! It is this weakness that allowed the cover-up of sexual abuse to happen. We need to rediscover how, before all else, we are equal brothers and sisters of Christ.

When Yves Congar OP challenged this clericalism before the Council, he suffered persecution. Asked how he was able to endure, he replied that it was 'le fait des frères', the fact of fraternity. Brother Bruno's profound understanding of what it means to be a brother to strangers is nourished by his own personal history which transcends cultural divisions, his father coming from Martinique and his mother being French.

One fruit and expression of this spirituality of fraternity is friendship, with others and with God. Blessed Jean-Joseph Lataste OP, a nineteenth-century French Dominican famous for his ministry to women prisoners, called the Dominicans 'an order of friends of God'. Because what binds us together is friendship with God, our preaching should point to God rather than to ourselves. So the preacher must be self-effacing. Bruno puts it beautifully: 'In the heart of all preaching lies that key moment when one must fall silent, withdraw, and let Jesus tread discreetly close in the silence ... The ultimate ambition of the preacher is to leave his hearers in conversation with Him whose very contemplation leaves him speechless.' People should be struck by the wonder of grace rather than by how wonderful is the preacher! We must get out of the way. After my first botched attempt at preaching, my student master, Geoffrey Preston OP, said to me: 'You used the word "I" too often.'

Of course our preaching passes through the prism of our humanity, our lived experience, our joy and sorrow. An impersonal preaching would be cold and dead. But like John the Baptist, 'he must increase, but I must decrease' (John 3: 30). So it is right that Dominic has never been venerated as the great founder, the one in whose shadow we live. When he died, the brethren were not particularly eager to seek his canonization. He was one of the brethren. His first biography is found in the *Vitae Fratrum*, 'The lives of the brethren'. This is the lesson that Brother Bruno lived as our Master, and teaches in this book.

This humility would be vacuous if it were not combined with a passion for the truth. *Veritas* is the motto of the Order, the truth of the Gospel, of God's grace and mercy, and the truth of what people live and suffer today. Bruno's eyes were opened to the 'underside', a favourite word, of the world during his time as a doctor in Haiti. Chrys McVey OP, an American who ministered in Pakistan for many years, wrote: 'Dominic was moved to tears – and to action – by the starving in Palencia, by the innkeeper in Toulouse, by the plight of some women in Fanjeaux. But that's not enough to explain his tears. They flowed from the discipline of an open-eyed spirituality that did not miss a thing. Truth is the motto of the Order – not its defence (as often understood), rather its perception. And keeping one's eyes open so as not to miss a thing, that can make the eyes smart.'

A humble but exigent truthfulness is urgently needed in our world of 'fake news', in which wild and unverified assertions are tossed out, expressive of subjective conviction rather than of objective fact. But it is a belief of the Dominican Order that even in this fog of 'truthiness', in the words of Stephen Colbert, human beings retain an enduring instinct for the truth which can be awoken when authentic words are spoken.

This is a spacious truth which we seek in conversation with people who think differently from ourselves, refusing the polarisation which is disfiguring the politics and even the religion of our time. Brother Bruno points out that Dominic's preaching began in his encounter with the Cathars, who believed 'it is possible to arrange good on one side, all evil on the other, and thus fix everything at once in in the world, in history and in human life': black and white, right and wrong, us and them. This is the blind and narrow antagonism which is tearing so many societies apart, and even the Church.

It is also a hopeful truth which refuses the fatalistic pessimism of so many. Bruno claims that it is 'the strength of the Liberation theologies to have shown that humankind cannot be robbed of its future because that future has a face, which is Christ's own.' In Bangui, the war-torn capital of the Central African Republic, he was told by a young Christian, 'You cannot kill the Resurrection.' This book is radiant with this hope.

Timothy Radcliffe OP

In dulcitudine societatis quaerere veritatem.
'In the sweetness of society, seek the truth.'
Albert the Great
1193–1280

PROLOGUE

This book has not turned out as initially envisaged: it was going to be a series of interviews with the writer and journalist Frédéric Mounier, whom I could not thank enough for the friendship, intelligence and patience he deployed to prise me out of my natural wariness. The arrangement of the themes discussed in these pages stems from his questioning, and the discipline he imposed on me sets me further in his debt.

The proposal from Les Éditions du Cerf was put to me on the occasion of the eight hundredth anniversary of the Order of Preachers. I overcame my reservations, challenged by the risk the exercise entailed and that I did not want to shirk. Would I be worthy of thousands of Dominic's brothers and sisters over the past eight centuries when bearing witness to our life choice, when expressing our faith using the words of today, and in keeping with the perils that threaten as never before the notion of humanity, the meaning of history and the future of creation? When persuading my readers in turn that the world has an underside, and that we must learn to listen to it with Him, the living Christ?

To these conversations with Frédéric Mounier, during which the story of my life as a friar preacher unfolded under his scrutiny, I owe the discovery of how crucial for me was this matter of an underside of the world heard out with Him. Who are you? asks the journalist. And there you go telling of a life in which you were hardly aware of the impact on your nature exerted by encounters and life events, hesitations and uncertainties, successes and – more important – failures. Here you are, amazed with gratitude for all those men and women who are your fellow travellers. Also, you discover, looking back, how and why the Order that you chose to ask to join has become the place where you like to learn to keep an eye open for God, to listen to and live by His Word. Which means that all sorts of reasons now crop up to prevaricate again, and relapse into that initial guardedness.

But now, at last, the book is here, which more than two years later, and towards the end of my term as Master of the Order of Preachers, translates our exchanges into a personal account. I cannot withhold the desire to express my deep gratitude to Saint Dominic and his Order, and with that in mind I want the book to stand as an invitation to dialogue with all those men and women who stand at the heart of evangelisation, and who seek to bear witness together to the hope that is within us (1 Peter 3: 15).

1

BECOMING A DOMINICAN

The birth unravelled

Who are you? I wish I could answer: a citizen of the inter-worlds. According to the civil registry office, by birth and by my native language I am a Frenchman, born in Le Creusot on 14 April 1954. But because my mother hails from Burgundy and my father from Martinique, I also perceive France, from earliest childhood, as somewhere else; a world that contains another world; an oddish blend that calls to mind all kinds of blends. My birth astride two universes directed my attention to the future of humankind: less and less did I ask myself where I came from, ready to leave that question unresolved, and more and more where I was going, careful to leave that question open. And I have applied that rule to anyone it has fallen to me to meet.

Even more than the power to draw from two different cultures, this awareness has fashioned me. The impossibility ever to know, as I traced my ancestry, whether the forebear I sought out had been master or slave caused me a fundamental disquiet, one owed not to a deprivation of serenity but to a lack of indifference towards what goes on around us. There has always been and always will be for me a world other than the immediate universe that appears to us to be secure and stable. Herein, beyond the good fortune of having multiple roots, lies the most essential lesson of my origins.

Mixed origins have their obvious side of self-transcendence, and a hidden wounded face. As a child in the playground, I happened once to be called a 'negro's son'. I can say that I made no great fuss about it; I cannot say that it didn't put me out. It left me, in my teens, totally unable to accept the sight of people stopped in the street because they were 'different'. To this day still, as an adult, I cannot stand being faced with such displays in the street or the Underground, where difference often leads to suspicion. Somewhere inside me rebellion smoulders, as if to say that it is not enough to oppose racism as the social scourge that it is. Rather we must stand up against the metaphysical evil that it is, first and foremost. A kind of Cain syndrome: the killing by real or symbolic murder of those whom Aimé Césaire called the *mendigots*, the lowest of the low.

My father roamed the earth, before finding his home base and family of choice. He had left Martinique, where he was born, to attend medical school in Paris before choosing to make his home in Le Creusot. It is pretty likely that he thus became the first West Indian doctor in that capital of iron- and steelworks. Some of his profession did not at first welcome his arrival, but they were to grow inured to his being their colleague. It also upset some among those who would end up in his care, while others seem to have recognized in this doctor from another world someone aware of their own wanderings from one culture to another. A strange but perhaps prophetic fraternity of the displaced!

We – my kin and I – aim to remain impervious to such prejudice. Back then, in metropolitan France, overseas cultural arrivals tended to blur particularities. Such authors as Patrick Chamoiseau, Raphaël Confiant and Dany Laferrière, thanks to whom we would at last discover the glories of island cultures, were, give or take a couple of years, my contemporaries. My father said very little about his origins, happy to summon them up by having us listen to Caribbean songs, or reading aloud from the speeches of Martin Luther King, or sharing with us his quip about the fact of time zones meaning that 'I got here six hours in arrears.'

Only later did I understand what Frantz Fanon meant when he remarked that you can take a child out of the country but not the country out of the child.

I was not to visit Martinique until I grew up, at the end of my tour of *coopération* duty[1] in Haiti, after my novitiate. On that land, finally able to learn Creole, I had the strange feeling of a joyful, life-giving intimacy in catching up with a language that could have been mine all along. In Fort de France, by paying a visit to a great-aunt I was meeting for the first time, I saw a family home. All this, by putting flesh, colour and smell to this maybe imaginary, undoubtedly invisible and unknown elsewhere to which I was no less bound by every fibre of my being, would find and internalize an essential driving force. Like a sketch of the Kingdom to come.

Located at the heart of the magnificent landscapes of the Morvan foothills, the unpretentious little town of Le Creusot, where I received my education up to the *baccalauréat*, offered a singular urban setting in the midst of transformation. The mining city of coal and cast iron, proud of the manufacture of the *Cristaux de la Reine* glassware company, had long since morphed into a metallurgical industrial centre. In imposing the supremacy of steel, the Schneider dynasty showed itself ready to inflict a paternalistic form of management that could also foster hostile

---

[1] The *coopération* was a system whereby students could delay their conscription for military service, serving a later and longer term posted in countries where their skills furthered the French government's development programmes.

labour disputes. But the steelworks' golden age gave way to a collapse of heavy industry. The world is mutating under our eyes. If it is not to lie fallow, to turn into T. S. Eliot's Waste Land, showing 'fear in a handful of dust', Le Creusot has to change, attract new businesses and convert the old deserted workshops into centres of cultural life.

The family home was arranged around the work of a general practitioner. My father did not begrudge his time, worked late into the evening, paid attention to his patients' ailments, whether true or imagined. My mother, apart from her housework, made the appointments, greeted the patients, consoled them if need be. Friends knew that the garage door was never bolted and that each of them might readily come in, after knocking three times on the lintel – the everyday features of a simple happiness. Anyone of a superstitious turn of mind who feels impelled to seek portents of what my life was to become is welcome to preserve the image of an open house of freely offered friendship.

Preserving childhood

Is the fact that my family were practising Catholics so decisive? I grew up in a world of faith, but not a faith that sorted people into believers and unbelievers. A family that bequeathed me its faith but that did not make its transmission compulsory. On Sundays my brother and sister and I went to mass with our mother; my father would only attend occasionally. In our parish, along with some friends, I served for some time as an altar boy. All the same, at the Schneider primary school, and then throughout my secondary state education, I rarely got involved with the *aumônerie*.[2] I was with the Scouts for a while, but only for a short while, because of their very controlling character, before joining the Francas[3] – the movement's secular counterpart, where for several years I enjoyed taking part in their educational project at a leisure centre. Within my family, however, never once was I asked why I was going here rather than there, or vice versa. This no doubt lies at the root of my lack of fondness for imposed codes and directed behaviours.

As Georges Bernanos liked to point out, the hallmark of childhood faith is its peace, its serene and joyful confidence. The irruptions of God into this tranquil ocean come as so many thunderclaps. Two moments remain engraved on my mind, from the first year of my secondary education. The first is of bliss, or

[2] The equivalent of universities' Christian clubs and societies. In France, religion is excluded from the curriculum; those wishing to pursue their religious practice do so in their own time through the chaplaincy provided by the local church.

[3] Somewhat akin to the Woodcraft Folk.

close to it, and followed a reading of the parable of the poor man Lazarus in the Gospel of Luke (16: 19–31), when the chaplain closed his address on these words: 'There was a rich man. There was a poor man whose name was Lazarus.' That the nameless one should not be the man one would naturally expect struck me as crucial then, and still does. The rich man, a show-off, has no name. The poor man, imperceptible, bears a name. This distinction has remained for me like a key to the Gospel.

The second moment came as a trial. Two girls from our class were killed in succession in road accidents. Faced with these tragedies, we were left completely at a loss, as if the brutality of their happening had stunned us – overwhelmed us. Now the same chaplain managed to make himself present to us, by making us present again to ourselves. He did not lard us with words and phrases in an effort to package what cannot possibly be wrapped up. He proved himself a genuine pastor – that is, quite simply, a witness. Another key to life in God.

It would take the passage of years, the fading, then revival, of these memories, before I could grasp that they signalled the finding of what Saint Paul meant by the word 'kenosis', that highest peak of divine love wherein absolute omnipotence deliberately manifests its radical powerlessness. But it would be a lie to claim that I heard it that way at the time. 'That, that's heavy, it's super-heavy!' the kid I was then told himself each time; and, all things considered, half a century later that phrase still seems fair to me to describe our encounter with mystery.

Thinking back on the young believer I was then, leaning towards faith and trusting in God, I would say that for that child the patent fact of the wonder of the world he was awaking to is inseparable from another wonder that lies within the first and dwells in secret there. A wonder more fascinating than all the wonders of the world, but one that has to be sought for, because through the power of what that great medieval Dominican Meister Eckhart might have termed its 'dazzling darkness' it calls us to itself.

Courting mystery

As a child, I wanted to care for children. At home, no one could conceive of a finer profession in all the world, but no one made it a requirement or an obsession. Still, my sister, when a freshly qualified nurse, promptly married a hospital resident, while my more offbeat brother ended up teaching in a veterinary school! As for myself, with good *baccalauréat* grades in the sciences, I headed for Dijon's medical school, a temporary sacrifice to the sacred duty that is the art of caring and, God willing, healing; but in my heart I harboured the dream of studying philosophy.

However, in the secret longing for a fulfilled existence, the monk's cloak quickly covered the philosopher's, when within me emerged the desire for a contemplative life – or rather when that longing rooted in childhood finally caught up with me. An existent place, also set on the underside of the world, was to show me how urgent it was. To some faiths you belong by birth, or adhere by choice, but in Christianity much is left to chance encounters.

Taizé is not an hour away from Le Creuzot. I was eighteen years old, and in that summer of 1972 the ecumenical community founded by Brother Roger, and where brothers and sisters of the Protestant and Catholic faiths share a life of prayer, was thriving. I had read its founding texts, but I knew nobody there, so I just turned up and, upon arrival, made for the church. I pushed the door open, stepped in, walked into its mighty nave and saw countless young people at prayer. That was for me the evidence of a close relation to God, of a connection made up of questioning and conversation as patently experienced and lived by those around me. So it was as simple a matter as that: being with Him to understand what prayer means.

I told my parents, tentatively, that I certainly felt drawn, and possibly even called, to the monastic life. Like many mothers and fathers pressed by their child to take a position on eternity, they chose to bide their time and answer: 'Yes, well . . . why not? But first complete your university course.' And so it turned out. Taizé had given me the taste for a personal relationship with God, for a contemplation set at the heart of the world, for a communion radiating beyond the demarcation lines. It spoke of a place open to all comers, where people come without reservation and without commitment – or hardly any. A place where all is undertaken freely, a way to be present to the Presence.

Discovering as an almost solid, tangible, palpable fact that there is an underside to appearances, a heart that beats in secret through the whirlwind of events, made itself felt as a grace amidst the working discipline I imposed upon myself. As early as the first Eastern anchorites whose rule was passed on to the West by Saint Benedict, work was understood as an antidote to illusion and acedia, those chronic diseases of the soul. The former amounts to belief in one's own self-sufficiency, the latter to wallowing in one's inadequacy, and both led introspection to turn into the cult of self. This is what is meant by the Apostle Paul's often misunderstood phrase 'not to let anyone eat who refused to work'[4] (2 Thess. 3: 10) – not to be understood as the harsh law of the exchange of labour for sustenance, but as the need to discard inaction in order to feed on something more than one's own petty self. As you give, so do you receive.

My Dijon years were austere. I discovered how much I loved my work, be it the intellectual challenge of the course of study or the practical demands of the hospital. I had set my heart on a residency and strove for it, earning with no small pride a place in Strasbourg halfway through my sixth year. Meanwhile, as the taste for prayer never left me, I was well aware of the difference between the student that I was and the monk that I was not – or not yet. This was not due to an ecclesiastical bent or an attachment to forms. But I understood quite simply that there has to be a clear-cut swing from before to after: a shift determined by the decision to admit to the insistent presence of a God one wishes to bind with to the extent of joining one's whole life to Him. I knew next to nothing then of the Dominican life; I had never come across it. But I knew that I had been baptized and that I was fully committed to fulfilling the promises made at my baptism, yearning to give more, discovering in study

---

[4] Biblical quotes are taken from the New Jerusalem Bible translation.

and care a path to prayer. A prelude to the world of Dominicanism?

Finding one's place

Was it that double rejection of both elitism and pietism that drew me closer to the Order of the Friars Preachers? It would be a bold assertion, dangerously close to the facile cultivation of false clues in hindsight, too often backdated into providential certainties. I was twenty-three years old, and so familiar was I with His presence in my everyday life that I always had the sense that something more essential was bound to take place with God. But what? That He alone should know the answer suited me fine.

My Strasbourg residency started, in the field of paediatrics. One half-year in child psychiatry, a half-year in haematology, followed by a year's paediatrics. Freudian theory on the one hand, clinical experience on the other, and a constant swing between the two. The consultants who guided me then taught me to cram, to endure and to listen. As my residency proceeded, the spectrum of my hesitations narrowed towards paediatrics, a holistic discipline where you have to learn to treat and to listen, both to the children and to their parents. One evening I attended vespers in a Dominican church. Do not ask why or how – I have no answer, and barely recall looking up its address in a telephone directory. What I do know is the nameless gladness I felt at once, in the company of these people who pray and preach, brimful of joy and freedom.

As my residency continued, my visits to this community, which numbered some twenty friars, became a sort of habit, like drawing breath. One thing led to another, and by means of some friends I mastered my shy reserve towards the place and met some Dominicans. A first conversation developed with one who was busy at the time deciphering the gnostic accents of *Life After Life*, the book by Dr Raymond Moody on 'near-death experiences' that had lately made its author world-famous. This friar wanted to consult with doctors or other medics who were only too familiar with dying for it not to have changed their existence – as was in part my own case – and we talked. A second meeting took place when during one of the bookshop crawls I relished I ran into another friar. This was Jean-René Bouchet, a deeply spiritual man who was in turn a professor of patristics, spiritual adviser to cloistered nuns and novice master of the Province of Toulouse. At the time he was Prior of the Strasbourg friary. In 1980 he became Provincial Superior for France before his sudden return to God seven years later. A lover of the Byzantine and Slavic worlds, he introduced me to *Requiem* by Anna Akhmatova, the Russian and female Homer of the century of concentration camps and charnel houses, and called to mind the healing power of the poetic voice.

The questioning of the tragedy of the world, and of its underside, which so inevitably turns to the bad, became painful during these meetings. Ivan's rebellion is famous, in Dostoevsky's *The Brothers Karamazov*, against such a God as allows the abuse and death of children. I was born in the wake of Auschwitz and the Gulag, which redouble the question. The hospital then became my teacher, tearing away the temptation to sleep, denying false consolations. Here is this small Moroccan boy who speaks no French and has to learn it, and whose lexicon's first word will be 'injection'. This boy who shares with me: 'My parents are afraid I'm going to die, you've got to help them', and then dies. This young man engaged to be married, who does not want to wed the love of his life because he does not want to leave her a widow, but who agrees at last to marry, and does not die. The ten-year-old lass who says to me: 'What do you want me to tell little Jesus for you?', then sees my bewilderment and adds: 'You know I'm going to see Him before you do.'

The mirage of willpower would have us believe we can build our lives as if to an architectural plan. All that has as much destroyed me as it has fashioned me. Or then again, it has fashioned me, but not without deconstructing the most uncertain, most useless part of myself, in an echo of Pascal's remark on the supposed power of reason. In this conflict between life which – simple and lucid – resists, and death which – misleading and often dismal – crushes, it is the dying who have led me, by preceding me, close to God. I thought I was accompanying them, but they were guiding me.

My time as a trainee therapist – that fine word that links the physician to the monk – taught me that all comes from God and returns to God, and that there is no human misery that can overcome the bliss of conversing with God, committing to God, and finding ourselves as nothing in the face of everything in us that stands with God.

I felt that bliss now and then, but never spoke of it. I sensed it among some of those Dominicans, but was not very close to them. The Dominicans, for their part, did not seek to recruit me – in fact they hardly sought my company. That is not their way, not their style. Yet one day, as I was skulking behind a pillar, one of the brothers came up to me and invited me to move up, which I understood as an invitation to take things further. Not long after that, I asked to meet the novice master.

It was not a decision. Or, if it was, it has to be understood as the decision I took to check with Him what to make of what I believed to be my path. In other words, that path seemed vital to me, but even more so to my close family and acquaintances. At the monastery, as I climbed the steps leading to the novice master's office, I came upon the friar with whom I had last chatted by the bookshop shelves, and who whispered: 'I have been wondering a while if you would finally show up.' Far from requiring some proof, in some way I had been begging for hints, and leaving others around me to drop them.

Back home in Le Creusot, I spoke with my parents again about the meaning that a consecrated life might hold, and they were wide open to it. Among my colleagues, when I mentioned the possibility of choosing such a life, two friends found the words I had been struggling for to state the glaringly obvious. At university, where I was completing my thesis on paediatric haematology on 'Leukemias with cells known as "of lymphosarcomatous appearance" in children', my thesis director reminded me on the occasion of my viva that a place had been kept for me in his team, and when he noted the lack of an answer to his offer, he went on: 'Whatever you do, may God be with you!' The next day I went to this noble figure of a man to explain that my trouble in answering him arose from my intention to enter the religious life. He honoured this confidence with an affectionate silence, and I knew then that the choice had been made. The moment had come to set the seal on it.

Accepting being a novice

I treasure the memory of my novitiate time. It is more than a memory. A religious commitment shares both with artistic or military commitments and with those of friendship or mutual love the indelible, incomparable mark left by the beginning. The word states that you are *novus*, 'new', but nothing prevents you from understanding it as the fact that you are re-newed, remade anew. For it says at the same time that he who is inexperienced is about to face what he has no foreknowledge of. How is one to find the world by losing it, given that this antechamber to the consecrated life is also a crossing of the desert that haunts us? The answer of our novice master, to whom I have never ceased feeling a boundless gratitude, was to plunge us into Scripture. The one decisive task, and the only test in his eyes, was to have read it at least once, from beginning to end, at a rate of two to three hours every morning. It was an exodus that revealed as an intense gladness the impenetrable aridity of the desert, especially when the flamboyant narrative of Genesis and the emotional imagery of the Covenant gave way to the cold namings of Leviticus.

As you walk through those immemorial scenes and landscapes, you grow aware that they are inhabited, that there is 'somebody' there, that He is a Word that emerges and speaks to whoever will listen. That is what Julien Gracq declares as he reads the Gospel and acknowledges in it the sound of 'an inimitable voice'. There he can be met, face to face, this Galilean whom deep down, I have to admit, I barely knew till then. But of whom a certain Matthew, Mark, Luke and John whispered to me that he is God come into this world, and that he addresses us, speaks to each one, giving to each their place, a unique one, in the history of His people. The tradition according to which the Word is incarnate both in the heart of Creation and in person, but also in Scripture, and that makes of the Bible a recapitulation of the universe and of history, holds good in that it transmits to each of us the responsibility to receive it in person.

The Bible is this place of *lectio divina*, the reading and prayer that come about in contemplation, in the inward gaze turned upon the invisible. But this same Scripture only makes all of its sense when it takes flesh within us. What flesh? The novitiate is also – is first and foremost – brothers, community, friendship, a true and free life, goodwill towards the world, a lovely celebration of faith, a word that announces Jesus, makes him present, reveals that that Presence will always prevail over the abyss. A Eucharist lived together like a passing into the Body of Christ within which we are brothers.

The life path of that Church Father who was also a Father of Preaching, John Chrysostom, 'the golden-mouthed', offers a model of this. In the fourth century this monk from Antioch became a preacher in Constantinople, for he understood that while the solid desert had become a spiritual city, with the blossoming of countless convents and hermitages, the real city, where the men and women of the common people dwelled, remained a spiritual desert. He took as his watchword that the sacrament of the altar and the sacrament of the brother are one and the same. Fraternity, with all its abrasive aspects, constitutes an essential part of Dominican asceticism, while at the same time it is an integral part of the proclamation that the Kingdom of God is at hand.

Does the blessing time of the novitiate arrive without longings for the world that is left behind? The dazzle of radicality has beauty on its side. It has temporality against it. That all things pass, that everything leads to disillusion, that nothing is deserving of eternity: this is the uncertainty towards which the *Diabolos*, the Gospel's Great Divider, tirelessly strives. Thus an urge becomes true when it is fully experienced, that is when we undergo it to the point that it strengthen us.

So yes, there is no crossing over without trial. What to reveal? The brutal realization that you will have no career, no marriage, no family, no descendants? That you will never be a doctor, never a paediatrician? That you will have to live within the world in the outlandish awareness of the solitude that you have chosen in perpetuity? That around you whirl the images of a life lived yesterday that might have been lived tomorrow? That the rackety bustle of the wards, the studious surroundings of the hospital school, the genuine, shared and mutual attentions with colleagues and with patients, the total availability that is both required of you and offered to you when you are on duty, the fact that, along with your team, you must confront sickness and death – that too was a vocation, and now you must give it up? The fact that it grows upon you that some among those that you love cannot love your life choice because they do not understand it? And that all this is not without its caustic side? Or worse: that the unlikely quest for holiness removes from you those moments of deep togetherness in adversity when for instance Matron, sensing your exhaustion better than you dare to, tells you: 'That makes five deaths this week. Perhaps you should take two days off?'

Under scrutiny, these 'longings' that are rooted deep in the past or projected into the future turn out often to be sublimated in the first case, and always fictitious in the second. It is as though they lurk in our minds, ready, like the fabulous creatures of myth, to burst out again at the least expected moment, like so many opportunities to relive the freedom of a choice. The truth is that all life is in the image of an organism shaped by gradual progression over time. It draws its freedom, growth and blossoming, not from achieving all its possibilities, but precisely by discarding those that are not to be, by drawing support from a few at the cost of the rest. The same goes for our own lives: behind every growing branch, there is a crop of wilted shoots. and this is all to the good, for therein lies the irreducible mystery of which every human being is the sign.

In my still vibrant memory of the novitiate, that year remarkable for its fullness was a turning point, wresting me out of myself to transplant me into the heart of Dominican life. It would bridge the gap between the residency where I nursed projects of a medical career, and the two years in Haiti that followed – an exceptional period that revealed to me how a 'Dominican project' could call me in ways far other than those I had imagined. That may be one of the tasks of a novitiate: it would set me on a path on which I never stop losing what I think is better for me to regain, going from founding moment to founding moment right up to the lavish baptismal restoration that is the clothing ceremony. As so many did before me, and will do after me, I entered the Dominican fraternity that would not be defined by my expectations of it.

Learning poverty

Following the novitiate, I had to honour the national service obligations that doctors often defer until after their medical training. I was twenty-six years old, and the time had come to leave the motherland, as also to part with old habits. The first posting considered was Guadeloupe, close to Martinique, where I could continue with medicine and practise paediatrics, accruing two half-years for my residency. Instead of which the Prior Provincial asked me to spend two years in Haiti with the Catholic Delegation for Cooperation (CDC),[5] an international service of the Church of France that sends over five hundred volunteers a year to more than fifty countries to assist with development. I was to rejoin the friars who form a small community in the world's first country to be born of a slave revolt. Shall I confess that I knew next to nothing about the Order's founding history of the first Hispaniola community that has since grown so dear to me?

The notification arrived, and it went unquestioned. I was given the chance to do at last what I could not expect and could therefore not refuse or debate. The leaving was peaceful, the arrival deeply moving. My first discovery lay with the very simple, almost

[5] This French NGO is an organization licensed by the state to send volunteers worldwide.

austere welcome, of the brothers and sisters; it was plain to see that, here, life spoke louder than words. The second, which followed close behind, involved the strenuous hardship of their mission. Located at the heart of the Artibonite Valley, a land of steep rock faces that stretches along its eponymous river, and endowed with a fine rebellious spirit, the friars ran a vast parish of the hilly uplands that the Creole tongue calls '*mornes*'. In line with their reading of the Acts of the Apostles, they created with the local people about a hundred base communities called fraternities. Their aim was to set up free clinics, train health workers and offer daily health consultations to be numbered by the dozen. In other words, they lived out with the people the beautiful, joyous and demanding reality of Brotherhood in Christ. I had left for elsewhere, and I found the Church.

My life from then on was nomadic. A friar took me to Tènet, a distant hill village, lost and magnificent, gave me a lesson on the way in Creole grammar, and then dropped me off with instructions to stay for as long as it took to master the language. At first, the locals thought I had fallen from another planet, and couldn't stop worrying about my love of reading. 'How's it going?' they asked, when they feared that I was bored. It went all the better because, by teaching me to speak their tongue with every chance encounter, they were to teach me to live in another way.

Soon I found myself crisscrossing the *mornes* on foot or on horseback, learning from them that you have to cut wood for the fire if you want to eat, economize on water it you want to drink, never forget to carry a bar of soap in case you cross a river and can wash. I find that 'Life is not sweet' as they say in Creole, but it can have the beauty of the fight to prevail over the obstacle. This frugality helped the travelling doctor I had become, handing out diagnoses, advice and treatment, to understand amid this hardship and desolation what he might possibly never have grasped back there in the hospital training wards: namely that the science learned over these years of study is not enough, here and with hardly any resources, to make the doctor effective and – most of all – credible. That you must listen before you auscultate. That the patient has three questions for the medic: why am I ill? How can I get better? What, or rather who, does my illness come from? I understand how this woman, whose baby refuses the breast and appears to reject this age-old act of motherhood, has every right to ask me: 'Has my husband sold him to a spirit?' before asking: 'Do you think you are strong enough to save him?' This rich applied experience, far removed from the textbooks, of what are, on the ground, the needs of primary care and issues of public health, does not detract from the spiritual lesson – received because unexpected – that comes with it.

It is poverty that I discover, inasmuch as it is vital to faith. It is in life that I discover life, as only the poor know how to pass it on. I do not educate them in hygiene, they educate me in life, and together we seek health. All at once, these landscapes, these friendships, bind me to them, just as we are bound by the place and background of our birth. Dare I write this? I lived there a Church life of extreme authenticity and simplicity the like of which I had never seen before and which, to my sorrow, I have not seen since. I saw in Haiti a different Church. I knew that it could exist. I grew convinced that it is just. The memory of that time past rules my dreams for the Church of tomorrow. It is not by promoting an institution that delivers sacramental services to the devotional consumer that the Good News comes. It is by preaching the Gospel that we communicate to others the desire to bear witness to it in fraternity, and that we enable the fraternities thus created to put their trust in God, who works at the heart of their history so that they may offer hope to the world.

The reading suggestions of a very wise and much loved brother, namely our superior, comfort me. I delve into the Documents of the Second Vatican Council, starting with *Gaudium et Spes* and *Lumen*

Gentium, and the subsequent encyclical letters, among them *Popularum Progressio, Ecclesiam Suam* and *Evangelii Nuntiandi*, not forgetting the document of the Third Latin American Episcopal Conference that met in Puebla in 1979. These key texts all put the question of an integral and united development of humanity in the light of God's plan. They all refer to a 'Sacrament of Salvation' Church. But mine is the school of practice, of confrontation with injustice and its crimes, dictatorship and its savagery, corruption and its havoc. These fraternities live in appalling conditions of forsakenness, contempt and oppression. And yet they act and actually build paths of hope, in spite of the militias, *tontons macoutes* and other lordlings in their droves, all of this against that singular background that the Voodoo culture creates. Under these skies there are nothing but disparate situations, each one providing a lesson, without a systematic frame of mind, but each of them shedding light on the Gospel.

'To anyone who slaps you on one cheek, present the other cheek as well.' We had just read Luke 6: 29 at a gathering in the *mornes*, almost the middle of nowhere, next to a hamlet that had become my second home, but where a greedy family was busy grabbing all the land at gunpoint. A young man stood up and asked everybody: 'They've taken a patch of my land. Have I got to give them another?'

The hubbub rises and spreads. Most of those present consider that he must not give in. They argue that he has to resist. I remain silent, not because I have nothing to say or because I am their guest, but because I am dazzled by the faith that gives them the courage to assert their inalienable right like this. Silent too because, perhaps like the wealthy young man in the Gospel, I had quite simply never seen things that way.

'In so far as you did this to one of the least of these brothers of mine, you did it to me' (Matthew 25: 40). In the face of another glaring injustice hitting humble people, another fraternity relies on this verse to take their case to court. For months, its members live through the procedural twists of a court action, from the denial of merit to the refusal to instruct, to the file lost by the deputy public prosecutor, to the judge's heedless absence. At last a date is set for the hearing. The night before, just as everybody is getting ready to leave for the town, a woman gives birth. In the morning the plaintiffs win their case. The newborn will be named 'Petit-Procès'[6] in memory of this collective birth of the act of fighting together for a just cause.

'And if one member suffer any thing, all the members suffer with it' (1 Cor. 12: 26). So went the heading,

[6] Small-Trial.

taken from St Paul, to a letter sent by one community to all the parishes of the island and asking them to oppose the dam an American company wanted to build, but that would flood the only fertile land the community owned. The movement grew, and in the end it won. Who will not praise a people that takes to civil resistance in order to make its dignity heard? But likewise, who will help?

Now violence is everywhere. I had, as did others, to suffer the threats that are certain to fly as soon you make the slightest move to thwart organized crime or petty brigandage alike. Later on, state violence compounded criminal violence, and unhappily friends were arrested and tortured. Some were eliminated, others had to leave the country fleeing death. How is one to halt this destructive spiral that soon leads to the conclusion that it cannot be borne? For all that I have never been a non-violent activist, I remain convinced that the spoken word can disarm hostility. When it becomes a shared procedure, because one group has been able to impose the exchange, the conflicts, interests and emotions involved express themselves differently, and are differently gauged.

But the fundamental lesson of commitment lies elsewhere. It is impossible to live an authentically human existence as long as one remains unaware of the intrinsic vulnerability of every man and woman, the frailty that no one is immune to, and the insecurity that can overtake any one of us at any moment. When this unawareness is deliberate, it injures the dignity not only of the poor, but of all of us. This, to me is what fundamental commitment should amount to: to defend the right of each and every one to belong to common humanity. Fraternity, always!

Obedience in patience

Concerning the Order in those days, I knew what I saw and lived through in Strasbourg and Haiti, and those early views delighted me. A little later, during a seminar that assembled the Dominicans of the Caribbean, I was constantly taken aback by the overriding clericalism of the discussion. Later still, at a congress held in Madrid, the reception given to my presentation on the Base Fraternities gave me to understand that the model was far from enjoying unanimous approval. It was at that point that the time came for me to return to France.

This return went less straightforwardly than might have been wished, but that was very likely my own doing. I lived with the idea of reviving, as a preacher, the life that I had just been through. I wanted to go back to where I came from – or to somewhere like it – to live a life identical or similar to the one that I knew. Paradoxically, France, the Church, the Priory, came as an ordeal of foreignness. At the risk of annoying my brothers by harping on my experience, I had no intention of keeping quiet about it. Seeking to prolong, at a remove, that fundamental experience with my Haitian friends, I was to have the opportunity during those years of study to involve myself a little with the Secours Catholique,[7] to campaign with Frères des Hommes,[8] and to form a few friendships with 'street people' whom I believe I saw as my 'guardians'.

The Psalms that are the way I see the poems of my Haitian friends within the fraternities revealed to me the actuality of the Word, at that crossroads where the history of God with men and women encounters their history among themselves. I understood, thanks to this experience, that the proclamation of the Gospel can transform human beings, transfigure the Church and change the world. While it had crossed my mind, of course, that someone, who is God, is present in that dereliction that touches the inmost core of the person, and hence of humanity as a whole. I might have suspected it before, but there I felt it, I would say, to the marrow of my bones. It is this experience of the

---

[7] The French branch of Caritas Internationalis, a confederation of Catholic relief, development and social service organizations operating throughout the world.

[8] A secular NGO supporting projects of sustainable development.

underside of the world, which gives an insight into its truth, that told me that my life would be Dominican through and through. Irreversibly.

All the same, my brothers had no intention of letting me leave again. They deemed their decision a fair one. Perhaps it was wise. It was certainly hard to take. Still, so be it. The year is 1983. I am sent on a one-year course in Strasbourg, with the Bible and philosophy on the programme. In the mind of those who decided it, this was to be a period of transition. For me it would be a time of loneliness. The brother they gave me as a tutor may have sensed it – I cannot tell – but he proved an extraordinary guide, gave me the companionship of books, and demanded that I go straight to the authors and shun commentaries in favour of the source texts. Among other shining encounters stands Emmanuel Levinas, the thinker of ethics as 'first philosophy', whose works have remained to this day my daily companions. Here again, the desert, even such a lesser one, fills with intangible presences and performs its work of regeneration. It was after this time of crossing over that I took my solemn vows.

The horizon of my vocation seemed so clear to me: to return to these places of fraternal solidarity out on the underside of the world. Once, twice, three times, I voiced the same request to go back, and once, twice, three times met with the same reply. It was no.

I thought at the time that I was not mistaken: that my life lay there, elsewhere, among the poorest of the poor.

But it did not happen. I was not going back to Haiti and was never to do so. Here, also, began the true affliction, and a hard one to endure – as it has to be, or else it would bear no fruit: waiting in patience, which comes from Latin *pati*, to suffer. The suffering that besets you and that you endure does not mean just a resigned perseverance; more than that, it elicits the virtue, which is also a power, to leave in place what one would readily remove, and thereby to assay a deeper freedom. A freedom that leads you on paths that you would rather not have chosen, yet without forcing you to forget what gave you life, for all that.

It was the brothers at our priory in Lille that I joined in order to complete my cycle of study, embark on a PhD in theology, and start to teach ethics at the medical school. So began those creative years that owed much to the constraint they entailed. It remains in my heart, and has not been erased but has in a way been transcended. It paled beside the gladness bestowed as I perceived the aptness of Albert the Great's saying: 'Truth is sought and is found in the sweetness of brotherhood.' How should I not say, at this remove, that religious obedience took me once again where I had no idea that I was able to go? It is this existential branching out that counts, because to spiritualize misfortune does not remove its hurt. It is through the brothers, the friends, and those around you that you overcome your outer resentment or inner division. They are the prop and the lever towards living out the vow of obedience.

This concept sometimes even becomes the object, in religious life, of an almost military discourse of the will that says nothing about its mystery and indeed stifles it. While standing at the threshold of the Order, each person may wish to take a path that they deem valid. By entering the Order, all may be led to serve other ways, and no less valid. Whether within the priory, the province or the General Curia, the friars strive to draw up the common plan for which they wish to assume responsibility together. After the grace of God, in order to truly obey they need the community, which is to say the apostolic encounter and apostolic communion for the sake of the apostolic good of the Order. Far beyond a 'will to obey' lies the desire to have oneself seized by the 'grace of an apostolic obedience' in which the brothers support each other.

I understood then that to desert the assembled community in its task was to desert oneself, for a preacher's vocation claimed solely as one's own is no longer backed by the others' support. This vigilance exercised by and for our brothers and sisters not only underpins the community, it sways the course of the world. Anyone's lot will heal or wound another's, and that gives us all common cause in the welcome of salvation. That, I believe, is what obedience is: to entrust one's calling to others. And that trust defines the Dominican life.

2

Being a Preacher

Embracing the future

So here I was, 'on mission', sent somewhere other than hoped. Once again, biographical landmarks matter little in the view of the symbolic events that contain them: one ought not to dwell on oneself. And yet these landmarks do make it possible to shed light on what the Dominican existence affords in itself.

My first years of study completed, I undertook a Licentiate of Sacred Theology, then a PhD in moral theology. That was a duty. Once my vows were taken, on the day of my ordination to the priesthood I became a student master, which is both office and ministry. I found my mission, in the apostolic sense that the Order gives it, in the world of bioethics. As Lille Catholic University was the only one in France that contained a medical school, I joined the interdisciplinary centre for research in Christian ethics now known as the Medical Ethics Centre. There I studied the methods of those great forerunners

Charles Lefebvre, Jérôme Régnier and the Dominican Sister Marie-François Lamau. I learned to teach and study in an interdisciplinary context. I discovered the joys and the demands of a research team. I learned how carers, practitioners and researchers conversed with lawyers, sociologists and theologians, and how a friendship both scholarly and human united them all, no matter what their standpoint. That apprenticeship was my mission.

Learn? There is so much to study in order to understand, at least a little, the new biomedical fields of knowledge, and to get to know the major theological and philosophical schools of thought that interact with biomedicine. Those years were studious, again, just as those that led up to my residency had been. So that meant study, to be sure, but also – and above all – learning to listen. I schooled myself in the power of listening, I practised the virtues of otherness. I immersed myself in the exacting sense of reality that research in friendship requires and presupposes. The rigour of ethics revealed itself to me in this dynamic of research, together with others, into the truth and soundness of an act. Whoever strives to master a branch of knowledge is always tempted – and by the same token the theologian, perhaps more than others – to think themselves sole owners of the truth, able unaided, and on the basis of that unique knowledge, to take full measure of the question they are facing. To the contrary, I experienced the welding – for that is the word – achieved by a research team that assembles specialists in diverse disciplines.

Respecting the other, dialoguing with the other, understanding the thinking of the other for what it is, in all its indisputable difference, provides an escape from the fatal presumption of totality, and a doorway into the living dialectic of truth. Becoming a brother, connecting as a brother – 'brothering', as one friend suggested to me – rather than making acquaintance with contemporary humankind, by building a genuine bridge to the culture they live by – this has been the Dominicans' ambition from their inception to the present, sometimes at risk of going misunderstood by the powers that be. It is the daring of Thomas Aquinas facing, in the midst of the thirteenth century, the Aristotelian revolution in cosmology, and at first being held suspect. It is the courage of Marie-Joseph Lagrange at the turn of the twentieth century, facing the renaissance in biblical studies, censured and silenced for a while. It is the conviction of the theologians who, at the time of the Council, dared to insist that it was possible to think together, and in a historical and critical manner, beyond the accepted models, in order to delve ever deeper into the mystery of the Church and the sacrament of salvation. It is the strength of some Liberation theologians who, despite the suspicions sometimes aimed at them, do not abandon their efforts to unfold as best they can the understanding of the mystery of Revelation and salvation, taking account of the plight of the world's most forgotten people. The tenacity of all of these nourishes the Church of today.

While I make no claim to match them, their example inspired me when I started my thesis in moral theology on antenatal diagnosis. The subject is difficult in itself, but above all rich in distinct, not to say contradictory, perspectives. It bears on the many mutations surrounding birth. It involves our relation to the techno-sciences, but also to parenthood, common concerns and life. This research took me not only to libraries but also to hospitals, both public and private, where I attended meetings and followed the presentation of the cases, gauging to what extent each decision yielded a response that raised as many questions as it resolved. What a schooling in humanity, to be able to admire the constantly exacting demands on the human person!

My colleagues knew that I was a Dominican; they were well aware that I knew the positions of the Church and could testify to them if need be. But I was not there in the role of official believer and cleric. For me, as for them, the question was not framed in these terms. I was there on the strength of my research in ethics, no more or less than anyone else. When I heard the members of these teams discuss cases, examine the alternatives, argue for the greatest possible good of the person, the family and society, debate over the respect and advancement of their dignity, I knew that I was taking part with them in constructing a magnificent history.

That is the way that research into ethics ought to go, underpinned first of all by paying heed to human morality in action. The temptation to lay down the law dissolves under the readiness to listen to what is being said about human trials and moral capacity, rather than to silence it. In the exchange of words, moralities communicate, truths are voiced and critiqued in good faith; they tolerate and mutually uphold each other in order to arrive at an optimal decision that favours the expression of full humanity, and thus the advance of human morality. The rules do exist, they do hold true, but the rules do not constitute the gateway. Dialogue replaces the 'thou shalt not' of belief based on certainty in favour of the 'here is why' of a faith in search of understanding. Only the sharing of reason among several makes it possible to seek the truth, to discover the good, and in the end to see a decision emerge that all can endorse.

Is this a surrender to relativism? No, for at the same time this does not involve laying anthropological theories in the scales and weighing them up against each other with a view to a pragmatic trade-off. On the contrary, it calls for piecing together the human factors, in order to identify and enlarge on what humankind is. Such an approach far surpasses the lowest common denominator that could by no means satisfy it. The sharing, together, of moralities summons up the highest expression of morality for today and its projection into the future. The condition of that sharing is reciprocal authenticity. Subjectivity is no kinder to systems of belief than to those of unbelief. Our opinions, rationales and actions carry their constant stamp in our everyday life, and it is indeed in this way that we fully become the human person that we are, unifying heart and mind. The beauty of humankind lies in being a creature both of reason and conviction, of objective rationality and subjective adherence.

That is precisely what we strove to achieve at Lille Catholic University. We developed what has to be called a clinical ethic. Not that the clinicians deliver findings to the ethicists that they have only to endorse; nor that the ethicists show up to examine and still less to assess what the clinicians do! Simply that those men and women who took the time to study the moral, theological and philosophical traditions also took the time to share their findings with those men and women who devoted their time to the practice of medicine, the provision of care, and to therapeutic thinking. And vice versa.

The aim was to establish, in common, a shared discernment. According to Emmanuel Levinas, 'The miracle of creation is to have created a moral being.' It is here that research in morality merges spontaneously into research in theology. Ethics, which Levinas defines as 'first philosophy', is also 'first clinical teaching' and 'first theology'. It was here that my Dominican self felt at home.

Speaking the Word

Ethical questionings were and always will be fundamental. As a result of the recent technological revolutions, today they assume a crucial character – along with the range of passions they entail. Rather than claiming who knows what expertise, wisdom or authority in the face of a supposed threat, whether grounded or imaginary, the question is to know whether the moral capability of humankind can speak out, no matter in what circumstances. Is it realistic to deem it possible always and everywhere? I say Yes. It follows that the same applies to the demands and concerns raised by the advance of the techno-sciences. It is this conviction that sustains the friendship in research. It underpins the harmony of researchers, in a common goodwill among all. It brings out the authentic figure of the human person in their search for truth because it is in their image. 'Where danger grows, there too grows what saves,' wrote Friedrich Hölderlin. The kindly wager on moral capability is for me a gateway to the contemplation of the mystery of that promised salvation.

This understanding is vital. It forces due heed to be paid to the indispensable contribution that France and Europe can make to what has become a planet-wide debate. North American research offers a wealth of prescriptions. More principle-driven and deontological, it puts forward numerous guides to making decisions. That is a feasible approach. It is not the path I have chosen to explore. What scientists discuss can make up people's lives. It makes known to them the very good reasons there are to confide in their moral capability. It trusts them with the historical concern to make and protect the world, rather than suspecting them a priori of allowing it to fall apart. As in biblical history, where the account is never straitjacketed into a single interpretation, such a narrative version of ethics, based on the story of a situation, is protected from relativism precisely because it refuses to claim the first and the final word.

The spectre of the jeopardy entailed in the present day's transformations haunts me, but basically I fear not so much the risks of a general laxity that would soon find its own limitations as the peril of a normative ethics bidding to take over. Behind this false absolute lurks the ultimate temptation of modern reason and its ambition to wield a total control over things, right up to the qualms of uncertainty, the undecidability of tragedy. It is plain to see how much this passion for domination can crop up in many scientific and technological fields. Indeed ethics is everywhere to be seen, because the question of human morality is present on every street corner. But then comes the risk of elevating ethics into 'ethicism', a sort of 'ethical magisterium' that would spare one the risk of thinking and acting in conscience, and of laying issues open to the good consciences of the moment.

In that risk lies the most clear and present danger, for in each human being lie elements of the indecisive, the unforeseen, of disarray. There is fracture and convulsion. It is thanks to this lack – and not in spite of this flaw – that a person can be trusted. The truth, the beauty and the goodness of humanity do not reside in the simple application of a set idea of what is good, beautiful and true, but stem from the tragedy of the human condition. It is through their own moral creativity that people can surprise themselves, that they discover that they are greater than they could or would ever have thought.

In Christianity, this risk can take the guise of a will to bring the Kingdom into being, at best to hasten its coming so that the world may end, at worst presuming to build it in human terms alone. But such a statement has only to be made to give itself the lie. The issue of faith, on the contrary, is to blaze trails and to build bridges in the world to welcome the Kingdom that is coming. The temptation for every man and woman is to dominate the world so as to order it, which most often means to cut it to our measure. Early on, in the confrontation with hardship, sickness and death, I felt this false and pointless yearning. It is in the heart of that chaos that, as ever, human greatness emerges, and that the expectation arises of a future that will not be the handiwork of humankind. The privilege the Gospel bestows upon the poor derives from the fact that, having nothing, they nonetheless still give much of what the rich cannot possess – they who appear to have everything. In prophetic and sometimes raging tones, an author like Léon Bloy grasped that the blood of the poor, because it irrigates the world, is one of its great mysteries in the sense both of enigma and of sacrament.

A heartfelt stroke of reasoning lies at the tipping point where moral creativity intervenes. Being Christians, we belong to the history in which we recognize the ultimate meaning in Jesus – the way, the truth and the life. It is from that fountain that the disciple longs to draw the strength of his existence. But in order to do so, he or she must follow in the path by which Jesus himself draws close to humanity, shares its joys and sorrows and listens to its doubts and anxieties. It is in this encounter that the truth of Christ's love for humankind blazes out in all its radiance, that love that wishes all to have life, and to have it in abundance.

In face of the world changing around and within them, faced with the evolving course of history and of their own destiny, nevertheless men and women are ceaselessly drawn to cross-question themselves. How can the tradition of Revelation that I was brought up with help me – this time in the shape of a kind of wisdom – to confront the situation I am in, display my dignity, advance my humanity? Thus is whoever seeks the truth of humanness constantly bidden to understand themselves. The situation does not override tradition. Tradition does not exhaust the situation. No one has final ownership of either, but each invites drawing upon the other. A like dynamic helps towards understanding that no one individual can create a wisdom for all. A grounding in tradition plays off against experiment in situ. Otherness is not distortion.

Narrative ethics implies a similar intersection of accounts – 'unconfusedly, unchangeably, indivisibly, inseparably', as the Church describes the dual nature, divine and human, in the single person of Christ – what is known as *synergy*. For Christians, the chronicle of human action is underpinned by the odyssey of the Revelation, of what the Bible tells us and gives us to understand of the Creation, the Alliance, of God's intervention in the falls and revivals of human beings. At the junction of those two histories can be glimpsed the image of the future of humanity, the outline of practical hope rendered possible by the promise of the Kingdom, the face of the Son of God. This convergence alone can lead humankind to enter at last into dialogue both with itself and with the divine. And this is the way the Revelation unfolds.

The Gospel shows, by relating it, what the path is (Luke 24: 13–35). On their way to Emmaus, two disciples speak to one another; they converse, going over the catastrophe of the condemnation, execution and death of Jesus, that immediate story that they know nothing about. They wonder if they were not mistaken, and what their life will be now. Then somebody appears whom they do not recognize. He walks up to them, he listens, and then in his turn offers the story of his own interpretation of Scripture in relation to the story of their own confusion in interpreting it. It is through the conjunction of these accounts that all at once, together, they are in a position to construct a common humanity. They stop to take it in. Only now does He, the Christ who possesses it because He is it and embodies it, point out to them the ultimate meaning of the truth. And then He fades from their sight, allowing them to devise for themselves how they are going to announce this truth without claiming ownership of it.

The worst stumbling block to this acknowledgment is none other than oneself. It is troubling to see the extent to which disorder makes and undoes us. How we easily accommodate it from without, how we struggle to tame it from within, by making peace with it both in justice and in kindness. This state of frailty, this disposition to fallibility, in other words the trial of our human and sinful condition, is an intrinsic part of moral experience. Following that path means accepting in advance the joy of our debt towards all who walk it with us. And the diversity of persuasions pales before the community of gratitude.

The adventure of ethical research in theology calls for paying heed to three imperatives: gambling both in trust and kindness on humanity's moral creativity; rooting oneself in tradition to enable oneself to grasp the here and now; and maintaining the dynamics of a narrative mode that opens the story to the irruption of another story, to the Word that wishes to be able to approach the world, make itself familiar to the world, enter into dialogue with the world. To preach is not to take possession of the Word but to allow oneself to be the sign of it. The preacher's first and ultimate sermon is their life.

Being at one with the call

Are we ever done, in our lives, with their twists and turns, surprises and offshoots? In 2002 my brothers elected me Provincial of France. It was an election that I did not, or would not, see coming. Having walked slightly backwards into the ethical adventure, I had found happiness in it and wanted to continue. After all, I enjoyed teaching, I had built up a research team, organized collaborative networks, drafted several collective projects, and I thought I had a few insights or ideas to contribute as a thinker and writer. Suddenly I realized that all this was going to stop. Not going back to Haiti, being appointed student master, then elected prior of my priory – all of these previous episodes I had accepted out of obedience, but this time, inside myself, I thought: 'This is not possible.'

Unless the Master of the Order were to formally impose this appointment, it occurred to me at first to refuse it: that it was my right and my duty, fraternally but firmly, to say no to the possibility. Then, gradually, the contradiction dawned on my mind. As a student master, I had lectured on the meaning of obedience. As a prior, I had laboured to stress its importance to the friars. Should I not apply to myself what I had taught and – more simply – accept what the Province called me to do, since it had led me to this point?

The brothers and close friends with whom I raised my dilemma agreed that a major break was at issue. 'You will see, it is afterwards that the Good Lord will help you,' it amounted to telling me. I knew the truth in that, but, like Job in front of his friends, I was not so sure the Almighty was that concerned with the minutiae He left to His people. I was gnawed at by the harrowing ambition to lecture, to publish, to gain a following, to promote to its full extent what health care means. This was the point when the 'Never again?' question struck me. Why had the Order once set me on a track that I had not wished, only to ask me the next day or thereabouts to forgo it?

Had I remained a layman, my life would not have carried the burden of compulsory obedience. Perhaps it would have driven me mad – whether in my pride in taking my work too seriously, or in the turmoil of continual dead ends pursued to achieve it. It would be misleading, and simply a lie, for me to assert today that all that it takes is to comply and the rest is plain sailing. It was not easy for me to obey. However, little by little, obedience has helped me to listen and to hear something new, not in me but of me and about me. It has helped me grasp the newness, not indeed of the unwonted matters involved in the new job, but of the unknown that the old self proved to be, the unthought part of it. The man who hankered for something else was not, perhaps, as right as he claimed or wished, and – more simply – as he certainly would have loved to be. Obedience? It shoves, pummels, shapes you . . . perhaps it frees you.

All at once, I had to plunge into the life of the Province with a complex personality, immerse myself and navigate inside it. This I did. I had to know how to make decisions, foster initiatives, deal with conflicts, no longer able to concur with each and everybody and to seek the common good. This I learned. I had to preach more and more in places where the word of explicit faith is more usual than in the academic and research circles that I happily spent time in. This I accepted. I had to account to myself for the way in which I received Christ, proclaimed and followed Him, even as I accounted to and for others. I tried. In order to have some success in this, to find some sort of happiness in living it. God's grace and the brothers' trust provided.

And yet, even though I had the immense good fortune to have beside me highly talented companions without whom I could have done nothing, even if the team they made up was wonderful and gave infinitely precious support, the fate the position entailed, which now and then ran off the scale, was often a certain loneliness that could prove hard at times. Within a world more basically ecclesiastical than I had ever known before, I found myself alone in a way unknown before. The position of provincial is singular in so far as you are both of and in the community, one among others, but you are no longer a member in precisely this sense: that every member takes to and upon himself what the provincial says, thinks, wants and expects for the sake of the common good of the Province. This raises one more trial of humanity: the realization that no human group eludes the laws of gregariousness, and that it must ceaselessly struggle to overcome them.

Much is made of the question of authority. Better to focus on what is involved in wielding it. What is a superior? When it comes to the religious life, this nominalized, comparative or even superlative adjective is an antonym, a word that has to be understood as the very opposite of its apparent meaning. Poor and mendicant like all of his brothers, the superior obeys in lieu of commanding them, for he feels bound up with them all. He tries to ensure that every one is acknowledged, accepted and backed up by the others. That each one hears the particular call that will enable them to exercise their vocation in harmony with the community. That each is aware that he belongs to it by his strengths but also by his frailties. The superior upholds the precarious nature of the link, for as in a family and as in the world, it concerns first of all, because it is human, a 'brotherhood of the lame', to paraphrase J. Patočka. The discernment the superior must practise has to do with this alchemy. He keeps watch over unity, listens to it and preaches it, so that communion shall reign. It is God who, through grace, will make something of it.

Only faith in the divine grace that all may partake of (Acts 14: 27) makes it possible to live in a spirit of resolution, relevance and kindness with oneself; and at the same time to rely on the constant reminder from the Order's brothers of the demands of the religious profession that the function neither adds to nor removes from. Even before we take our vows, we Preachers ask for the mercy of God and of the Order. In this way we confess that mercy is not an additive that comes to make up for or amend our failures, but God's charity, which, from the very start and at every moment, is present to birth us to our true life, including our faults.

This above all is what it was given to me to understand over the course of my two four-year terms of office. In the depths of the person, the extreme richness of the experience, diverse and surprising, was there to make up for the tough or arid times of the position. But on the path of the Dominican there remained the constant of the vocation: as I reached the end of my term of office as provincial, again I faced the questions usual for any friar. What of the next stage? Would I go back to teaching or research? At long last go abroad again? Or would my next superior ask me something altogether different? Whereupon, on 5 September 2010, I was elected Master of the Order. I had thought I could rule that out, but it was poor forecasting. And as before, it was already too late to rejoice in or lament it. It was therefore a matter of continuing to try the fact that what we live through changes us without affecting the basis of our being, which remains in the hand of God. To be a Dominican means wanting to place one's intelligence, will and heart there too.

Serving the servants

When people sometimes write to me or address me as the 'Most Reverend Father General of the Friars Preacher', I answer that this title may well belong to another age, but more important, that it is inaccurate. If any superlative term of veneration and piety were appropriate, it is the Order that ought to be called 'most reverend', which is the very thing that it rejects through having decreed itself mendicant from its foundation. If the Master of the Order is not termed 'general', it is because there is plainly no question of commanding an army, but of the primary task requiring the Order to keep the promise summed up in contemplation, study and fraternal life, with a view to preaching. If the Order is indeed the Order of Preachers, which is to say of the friars who have given it their lives, it also numbers nuns and lay persons, sisters and priests, who all belong to the Dominican family, more vast than commonly assumed.

Failure to take these dimensions into account sunders the mission of the Master of the Order. At no time, incidentally, did the charge ever entail any supreme, pyramidal or immediate authority. It is more than symbolic but is not essentially concerned with hierarchical power. It supposes as its first and final duty to prevail upon the Order to stay united in its vocation. It is a matter of what Eastern Christianity calls a 'smallness', a way of life compelling modesty because it deals with serving those men and women who serve.

The Master of the Order, 'successor to Saint Dominic', is thus the agent of the Dominican communion and finds himself bound by this communion. We make a vow of obedience to remind ourselves that it is vital for us to help one another to listen in unity to the Word that Christ imparts to us and sends us to preach – so that the venture we undertake together has in its view the visible achievement of an ecclesial family devoted to the proclamation of the Kingdom. We have asked to become preachers in order to be given over to the Church and to the world as an emblem of the living Word. Herein lies the sole reason that keeps us together. The task of the superior, at whatever level, is to ensure that the conditions be met for this mystery to become – with a difference in scale – a miracle: here local, there global.

I have found myself asked whether such an office is not crushing; whether such a vigil did not keep me awake at night. Never effortless, nor always funny, this service is first of all a grace. It consists in receiving in trust the Order that was entrusted to you. For nine years on end, brothers, sisters, lay Dominicans from all over the world, amounting to as many singular people, different cultures, diverse sensitivities and experiences in faith, have demonstrated for you what it means to be a Preacher. This multiplicity of gifts within a unique vocation leads one to wonder what Dominic wanted, how to be faithful to him, and by what means his intuition is to be expressed nowadays. What is this institution which brings all these men, all these women, in vastly diverse places but with the same desire to proclaim the Gospel as a place where God's friendship encounters men and women's thirst for truth? The Order is by no means a preacher industry or sermon factory. It is, in the words of Blessed Jean-Joseph Lataste, an 'order of the friends of God'.

Banal though it is to say so, the conductor is nothing without the orchestra. It is fascinating to observe how those sisters and brothers, each and all of them so different, build one and the same Order. It is moving to note how their relationship with Jesus – Word and Truth – is with this one more exuberant, with that one more timid, but always personal. It is exhilarating to explore how the communities they form invent and reinvent themselves in accord their with European, African, Asian, American or Oceanian worlds in a quasi-sacrament of the communion of peoples and cultures foretold in Scripture. It is overwhelming to listen to them and to feel oneself bound up with them.

Particular individuals tell me about the life paths they believed they were choosing and on which they have in fact been sent. They share with me their presence within places of worship and parishes, in spaces of contemplation and of ongoing action, in cloisters, universities, laboratories, administrations, hospitals, prisons. They live in town centres or on the outskirts, in the heart of inner cities, open country and deserts. They meet couples and families, students and the elderly, sick people and prisoners, the poor and the rich, dropouts and decision-makers, those born into wealth and children of the street. They stand alongside affluent peoples and oppressed nations, on the frontiers, the demarcation and conflict lines, and even in those far-off corners of the world where they are the only Catholics in dialogue with unknown universes.

Each and every one tells me the singular stories that enthuse and upset them, their dreams and their anxieties for those men and women with whom they share their faith, their joyful and sorrowful passion to encounter humanity in all its conditions, to allow themselves to be inspired, as Dominic wanted, by the way in which Jesus wanted to bring himself close to all of us, to allow themselves to be marked by the seal of God's friendship and joint solidarity in the same promise of salvation. They tell me again how much this salvation is not theoretical, that there is no ideal preaching addressed to an ideal hearer, that grace occurs among tears and smiles.

So goes the thread of my days, which often leaves me voiceless. This is what I do: I see my brothers and my sisters each to their own measure, passing through life, or rather wishing to have Jesus pass through their life. If the Preacher has a secret it is that of being human, truly human, and from the depth of their humanity, to dare speak of God who made himself one of us, not in the fictitious glory of humanity but in its real hardship, in its lower depths and underside. My brothers and my sisters teach me how the human is a miracle.

3

Living the Order

Revisiting the beginnings

Is there such a thing as Dominicanism? Certainly, but it is not like a fixed essence dwelling in a never-changing sky. In order to grasp its true constants, which do not make axiomatic phrases, we must return to the beginnings.

When Dominic started to preach, around AD 1206, he confronted the 'Cathars' or Albigensians who embodied a major temptation of the religious mind and hence of human life: the belief that it is possible to arrange all good on one side, all evil on the other, and thus to fix everything at once in the world, in history, and in human life. Now when the disciples asked Him: 'Lord, do you want us to go and weed out the darnel from the field?' (Matt. 13: 24–30), the Master kept to himself the time to sow and the time to harvest. Discarding all a priori, preconceived ideas and ready-made judgements, Dominic wished to announce the Good News of the Kingdom as

Jesus had done, seeking people out as they were, and befriending them, starting with the poor, the ignorant and the sinners. This friendship is the first original guideline.

Now, it was women whom Dominic first dealt with on the path he chose, and as it happens women leaving Catharism and returning to the Church. He answered their plea, took them with him, but rather than taking them to preach in his company, he set them up as a contemplative community. They would be nuns living the message of salvation in prayerful silence, displaying the mission's ideal from within the cloister. Out of this first and unusual encounter sprang the conviction that contemplation dwells within preaching. This is the second guideline: the only certainty is that without inward conversion, and keeping a patient watch for Him who is to come, apostolic action remains futile.

Brothers now flocked in, ready to take holy orders, and others, fewer of them, who did not feel called to the priesthood, laypeople wishing to support the spread of charity, sisters called to bear witness differently through service. Dominic recognized that he had to proclaim the Kingdom with those men and women who came to him. They were to say together that the hope of the Creator was seeded already in his Creation, that the communion they were forming prefigured, signalled and secured it. Men and women, contemplatives and apostolics, priests and laypeople: this gathering was necessary to allow for 'holy preaching' to take on its full meaning and full scope. The definition of the Dominican family followed its formation. In this, its third fundamental guideline, it does not stand apart from the Church.

In wishing to define the Order, we end up telling the tale of an amazing adventure, in so far as it surprised and joyfully outdid even its own protagonists. In this respect, the context is never accidental. The period during which Dominic lived and worked was going through deep changes. The feudal system was on the wane, towns were restructuring themselves, the University was taking shape, the faithful took on an evangelical zeal, the clergy bristled under their critique.

How was the Kingdom to be proclaimed amid the ups and downs of this mutable world? To be sure, Dominic wanted a contemplative order which, in the eyes of the world, would hold at heart the mystery of the Word. But he also wanted an apostolic order that spread the Word in tune with the preaching of Jesus, in the midst of the world so that the world too might be in the midst of consecration (John 17, 18). So Dominic did not invent an Order; rather he rediscovered it, as Pope Honorius III confirmed on 18 January 1221, stating that through the Order: 'He who never ceases to fertilize his Church with new believers has wished to suit our modern times to those of its birth and to spread the Catholic faith.'

In an apparently surprising way, Dominic gathered men and women around him. But is this that much of a novelty? Women are at the core of the Gospel, that first text in human history where the humblest among them appear in their own name without needing to be aristocrats or heroines. Furthermore, his were the days of courtly love, that is to say of a culture of feeling that overrode the primitive rule of sexual domination. He himself endowed this transformation with a spiritual meaning.

Dominic readily took in all kinds of dropouts and their like, whether outcasts or religious rebels. His time is marked by lay-driven movements of renewal offset by revolutionary and mystic overtones. Now here too Scripture predominates. The Gospel decries the false public order, and the Acts of the Apostles did not understand ministries as a ruling clergy but rather as services helping the assembly of the 'saints', the believers, to evangelize (Eph. 4). These movements appealed to Dominic, he who was riveted by the imperative to work for unity. In his view, the movements must not divide the Church, but neither must the Church reject them. His solution relied on the twin adoption of those forms of extreme demand: that of mendicancy, in order to assume poverty, and of travel, so as to fulfil the mission. These measures do not amount to a method, but they have an end of their own, namely truth, the truth that 'begs' people's hospitality.

So, following Dominic means following him who himself follows Jesus, the first preacher to go in poverty from village to village to announce the Kingdom of God. Which means going in turn to join the people of the present day in the place where they are, meeting their thirst for communion, taking the promise back to them in the condition that is theirs. The place where God is acting, in the humanity of every man and woman, as also in the building of human relations. Dominic espoused radicalism – not the fanaticism the term conveys today, but in keeping with the word's very etymology: the quest for the root without which there is no growth or blossoming. So that the human word might truly lend itself to a conversation with God, he thought it crucial to go to those who either did not know the Church, or misjudged or rejected it.

Now in the effervescence of these movements caught up in the impatience of conversion, there appeared communities of penitents who would in due course form the Third Orders who would enrich the mendicant orders with the insights of their secular faith. These exchanges would rule out the lure of condescension. At the same time, Dominic no doubt foresaw that this radicalism, taken too far, might veer into the ideology of purity, then of purification, and finally of purge that would crystallize the spirit of schism, then of hostility and eventually hatred. That must be transfigured, and urgently. This would be the very specific role of study as a discipline, on equal terms with prayer and common life.

Each one of those aspirations holds quite as true today as it did then. To preach the Gospel radically, and fully to serve the Church: these are the two facets of the communion that Dominic instituted from the outset as the profession, so to say, of the Dominican.

Embracing history

Later, it has to be said, like every human entity, the Order faced the temptation to make itself a tool or accomplice of self-professed masters of the truth. This pitfall was tragic, because brothers were to take part in a system, the Inquisition, which sought to impose communion by means of dreadful campaigns of exclusion. Now, communion, in the Church, refers to the very way of being that exists in God the Father, the Son and the Holy Ghost. Its synonym is freedom, which itself excludes constraint, violence and submission.

Certainly, Dominic had no dealings with the Inquisition, which was instituted after his death, and cannot be imputed to his vision. Certainly, the episode requires to be set in its context. Certainly, the scholarly lessons that can be gleaned from the past always display a more complex picture than the hindsight models do. It is clear that in order to avoid anachronism, it is no bad thing to consider the time it took for humankind to postulate, notably in the case of Native American populations, that all human beings are equal no matter what their origin or colour. Or the time it took to abolish slavery, including in countries whose constitutions professed to be democratic. Or the time it takes, today, for every human person to be fully acknowledged in their rights and their dignity, without distinction of gender, social standing or cultural rank. The time it will take for tomorrow to correct the failings of the hyper-economy of globalization that ravages the weakest. The time and the energy it takes humans, ever and again, to banish all instrumentalization of humans.

In the course of several research symposiums, the Order's historical institute has devoted itself to a broad and rigorous study of the days of the Inquisition. These academic papers were not intended to be circulated, but it would be good to make them public. The fact remains that Dominican friars were party to the unsavoury episode of the Inquisition, that they involved themselves – some of them convinced of their good faith, others devoured by ambition, but all blinded by a form of pride. Today we judge this aberration unacceptable, and yet we did commit it. Along with so many others, we asserted: 'I myself know, and you do not. You must convert to what I say, for I know better than you what is good, just and true for you.' We cannot hide our faces. It happened just that way for us.

Yes, it took time for us to rid ourselves of the idea that somehow there was any kind of link between human power and the relation to God. We know now that under no circumstances can there be a link between the human will to exert control over other humans and the human desire to relate their existence to the life of God. A person is readily tempted to believe, or to have it believed, that they are greater than themselves, to legitimate their craving to master and subjugate the other. In this they re-enact the original sin: the notion that it always takes more power, and that they themselves may appropriate it, and claim to do so in God's name. In itself, this error has always signalled a very great aberration, and remains to this day a major temptation.

Although having received the inordinate trust of partaking in the Order of Preachers, we have not always lived, spoken and acted in keeping with the Word that we wished to preach. The critical accounting of this sombre period has accordingly a rightful part to play. It puts us on our guard against the slightest collusion between the seeking of truth in the Word and the power drive that holds sacred that intention for its own purposes of domination. Which extends beyond the case of the Inquisition. Henceforward, our general idea amounts on the contrary to saying that we must stand humbly before God. Such was Dominic's original intuition.

That is why, on the occasion of the Order's eight hundredth anniversary, we chose not to privilege a particular act of repentance. At the heart of the jubilee celebrations, we wished rather to mark our conversion – always aimed at preaching. It alone can consolidate in us an attitude of humility before the mystery of truth, and teach us to distrust the slightest temptation to exercise any sort of power in the name of our Preacher status. We decided that in 2016 Ash Wednesday, the day when, from earliest tradition, the pope celebrates the beginning of Lent at Santa Sabina, our mother church, would be dedicated in all our communities to a prayer of conversion. That that prayer would be the occasion to review our past and our present and to ask forgiveness for all that could have led to the belief that the human word concerning the Word mattered more than the Word itself. How could it go unnoticed that, by an act of providence, that same year was also an Extraordinary Jubilee of Mercy in the Church?

For conversion is indeed the stake of the Dominican fraternity, achieved through life in community when entered upon in truth. This project of fraternity offered and received, which lies only in mutual support, is that the sweetness of such a gift ends up adjusting each party to itself, soothing the hearts of all, defusing the recurring temptation of power in this world. It is true that this approach proves arduous at times, that it does not always yield the outcome hoped for, that it can stray again and again into formal practice. In short it is subject to our human contingencies. But herein precisely lies the Dominican venture: daring to believe that He, the Christ, can transfigure our attempts to build more and more every day, and more soundly, a truly human community, dedicated to listening to the Word, living by it, proclaiming it. And that it is through embracing history, in all of its lights and shades, that perpetual self-conversion persists.

Upholding unity

A small church working in the heart of the Church. A positive recollection that the Church of Christ is founded and grows to the extent that it preaches. Communities that seek to live out what they announce within the world. People of all ages, all origins and conditions, devoted to the Good News, who also suffer trials and setbacks, who know that the grace of fraternity is received in this imperfection, and that pathways to holiness can be glimpsed here. All these things that Dominic wanted form his posterity today. In other words the mystery that Paul had spoken of already: the treasure of the Gospel held in fragile earthenware jars (2 Cor. 4: 7).

Seen from without, no doubt it may prove hard to convey a definite model of the Dominicans. You seek in vain. Scholars or pastors? Intellectuals or pragmatists? Progressive or traditional? They are all these at once, and many more besides. It is the Order's wont not to attach importance to it. All have the right to be what they are, to think what they think, to bring shades of meaning of their own, to witness to their way of hoping in humanity, to love the world, and in this every personality has its due. In and by itself, the Order cultivates that possibly pretentious, certainly ambitious dream that God created manifold a single humanity, so that it might unfold its possibilities in the passion for the Word.

The irreducibility of vocations also helps to meet the urgencies of preaching, ever the same, ever different, which would otherwise lapse into human verbiage, a solipsistic drone. In itself, the Order helps each brother as best it can to fulfil that dream, to rejoice that each of his brothers entertains it, that such and such a brother, on the strength of his history, his sensibility, his training and his personal relations, proclaims the selfsame Jesus differently, that this goes for all of those he has been given as brothers, and that he may rejoice in it. It is the being diverse that engenders the becoming together.

Which may make the Order seem anarchic. It has been said, and we say it among ourselves from time to time. The Dominican family would like to be perfectly insubordinate to the law of the world, but realism must prevail: in every family, the temptation of some is to think themselves at the centre. It is the syndrome of the most senior, who think themselves the best interpreters of tradition, indeed its owners, or of the youngest, the most gifted, the most active, who deem themselves indispensable. That some should reach the point of wanting to make their own self-valuation, regardless of the rest, simply emphasizes that only a shared exactingness and joint responsibility make it possible for the apparent disorder to be somehow recalled to Order. It is more easily said than done, but here the whole matter appears, namely the joy of spending our life together as Preachers; the sheer craziness of believing that God is willing, through our words, to have his own heard; the surprise of seeing communion transcending differences.

The condition that permits this perpetual miracle lies with ourselves living truly what unites us. It means understanding that the first place in our preaching dwells within our own communities. Brothers must hear brothers speak of God out of their own contemplation, their studies, their actions, but also out of their personal experiences, their encounter with Christ and their life in the Spirit. If the Order were only a school of preachers trained to speak to others about God while remaining silent about God among themselves, it would lack the essential. That something – or next to nothing, but vital – that consists in saying: 'I struggle to understand how he lives, to grasp his theology, to accept his standpoints, but when he speaks of Jesus we speak of the same mystery of grace and the same promise of salvation.' It is up to me to relate to him, up to me to exchange with him, up to me to discover what he has discovered about Christ and that I do not know. By dint of listening to each other speak together about the Son of God, we are going to become better students, or rather friends, of Him whom we preach about.

The true threat would lie on the contrary in the volition to construct a polarized identity. That risk haunts our world today and does not spare Christians. This is why what the Order says about its unity concerns the whole Church and the revival of evangelization. The abounding wealth produced by the open acceptance of diversity is borne out most of the time, even if often despite ourselves, in ways other than we would have thought or desired. The fact is that we are all embarked on the same voyage and that there is only one harbour for all. Differences in attitudes, ideas and expressions are not annulled, they are preserved the better to be transcended.

With each Dominican, another planet that has to be guarded as a treasure. It is here that we have to stand watch. The common transition is provided by the Order for our common sanctification. Our brothers are akin to guardian angels who lead us on the path of God's friendship. They are our own evangelists. This is no slogan. We are preachers because we are brothers.

Cherishing otherness

The widespread notion according to which the Dominican family is organized into concentric circles with the friars in the middle, nuns in the second ring and laypeople on the outer ring is simply mistaken. It is also abusive, conveying worldly biases that do not belong in theology. That it is crucial to acknowledge the identity and the proper mission in the Church of the religious I do not doubt. It is always with emotion that I think of our six thousand brothers present on every continent, for the most part ordained to the priesthood and called to administer the sacraments.

However, there is no ignoring the fact that some of them are inclined to think that they alone matter. Now as one among us recently observed: 'We are brothers in the Order of Preachers, not members of the Order of Preacher Friars.'

Today, this challenge has grown. It is not easy for the churchmen that we are to accept the self-evident fact that the clergy are no more the centre of the assembly than they are of evangelization. But were they ever so, but for a fallacy made feasible by sociological circumstances? The centre is Christ, and His desire that all should be one. When He says that He is among us, He understands this 'us' in the irreducible diversity displayed by any human community. How, in our turn, are we to come to terms with this?

The temptation exists, which no clergyman avoids and which it is every clergyman's duty to flush out. It consists in thinking that your position as a man and as a priest renders axiomatic what you are going to say, that the attention that you enjoy places you at the centre of the world, that to have made a worthwhile remark one day grants you for ever the right to speak with authority, even if words should happen to fail you. The temptation is to believe that it falls to you to tell others why they must agree with you, whereas we are all of us called by Him alone. And to Him alone belongs the only true authority, whose proof is that He wields it in utter humility.

Since the beginnings of the Order, living out a true equality has amounted both to a wager and to a challenge. This holds good for the relations between veterans and newcomers, old and young, priests and laity, but even more primarily between men and women. It is not whistling in the wind to point this out. At the heart of the Dominican family there are more than 2,500 sisters, contemplative nuns who live in one or another of the 200 monasteries they have founded in the four corners of the world. Church law recognizes the autonomy of every enclosure in enshrining by statute its relations with the Holy See and the local bishop. But a further particular link is added in the case of the Order of Preachers. In line with the specific history and in view of the specific mission of the whole body of Dominicans, these nuns have as their regular superior the Master of the Order to which they are professed. Just as he has charge both of the friars and of the laypeople and the priestly fraternities – all direct members of the Order – the Master must see to it that the Dominican intuition is carried out in these monasteries. But here too there is no question of hierarchy. It is communion that rules in the perpetual shift between who gives and who receives.

The contemplative life of the sisters, in cloister and in silence, is the crucible of intercession for the world to which the Order was sent to preach, and for the Church that is built through proclaiming the Word. At the hub of the itinerant adventure of preaching, their monastic choice recalls that the heart stands watch there, and awaits the coming of Him who was the first itinerant teacher, begging for the hospitality that humanity could offer to God. So the sisters pray 'for the preaching', not only for those who preach but for those that they will preach to; and more broadly for the movement of proclaiming the Kingdom that underpins the evangelizing Church, that it may kindle in the world the flame of the eager vigil for the advent of God's truth. And their prayer confers with their study, since for the nuns, as for the Order overall, study is one of the chief observances. Thus the quest for the one truth is fulfilled in the diversity of charisms.

There is a very great complicity between the friars and the nuns, which harks back to Dominic's original intuition and to the foundation of the order. Dominic's nuns came into being a full ten years before his friars. They thus enjoy a kind of precedence in the birth of preaching. This pre-eminence is crucial, for it goes to show to what extent contemplation is the wellspring of the preaching. Cut off from its mystical retreat, the word emerges empty. 'Silence is the father of preachers,' we love to say. It is thus that the cloistered sisters of the Order keep the brothers from straying far from this imperative of truth, even as the risk of makeshift is permanent.

To the lived-out otherness that lies at the heart of the Dominican family, the apostolic sisters likewise bear witness. Most of them came later, during the seventeenth century, on the initiative of women like Marie Poussepin, and many congregations have sprung up since then. Many women were at the birth of spontaneous communities that enlisted beside or within the Order, having found there the very essence of their vocation. When institutionalizing themselves, they asked to be incorporated into the Order of Preachers, and are members of the Dominican family. They preserve their autonomy, but are part of the corpus of preaching presided over by the Master of the Order.

These congregations grew up within a great diversity of statutes, outreaches and structures. Some are small and local, others imposing and international. Today they number some 150, amounting to about twenty-five thousand sisters. Each one is organized into provinces, under the authority of a superior general. The great majority belong to the association of Dominican Sisters International whose co-ordinator is based at Santa Sabina in Rome. In their role as apostolic

Dominican sisters they represent an inseparable part of the Dominican world.

The apostolic sisters arose out of founding intuitions related chiefly to services of education, health, and of nearness to people and families, in particular those on the fringes of society. In this way, from the seventeenth to the twentieth century, they have taken part in many decisive advances relating to the status of women. They promoted the recognition of their equal dignity. They hastened the progress of their involvement in study and in professional life. They furthered the specific attention that I see paid by women to a just construction of society, and to the necessary ordering – likewise a special concern – of the priorities that must shape it. They also took a greater and greater part in the venture of theological studies.

Today as yesterday, all of this makes them a powerful presence. The status of women in society has changed. The way that women position and understand themselves, the way that they act within the Church, has also changed. Here a profound transformation is going on, spurring the thought that the very nature of women's apostolic life will have to transform. The stakes are all the higher because this form of consecration, which is to say commitment and witness, is essential to the mission of the Order. Not to fall short here would incidentally display a pure and simple faith with Dominic's original vision.

Rejoicing in diversity

There are so many ways to live the Dominican family life! Laypeople, first of all, present beside Dominic from the beginnings of the Order. They are now regrouped into the 'Lay Fraternities of Saint Dominic'. Based on the same three pillars of our observance, the lay Dominicans total about 150,000 in the world. They choose to join a fraternity that numbers from six to some twenty members and come together in prayer, study and meeting, sharing the light of faith in the melting-pot of their human experiences. Heirs to the Third Order, these fraternities belong institutionally to the Order and are linked directly to the Master. While they have their own structures, they do not make up what would amount to a 'movement of Dominican inspiration', but are indeed a communion of persons who wish to be part of Dominican preaching, are its agents and make up its promise.

Strong in their social, professional and familial life experiences, which represent for them the first site of evangelization, these laypeople offer in common their apostolic commitments to the Church – and all of this in ways that vary according to the country, in linkage with the local cultures that likewise form the mulch of their actions. They bring life to parishes, spiritual retreats and Bible study circles. They practise works of mercy, visit the sick in hospitals and students in schools, house street people and accompany migrants. They proclaim the Word on social networks. Some of them teach theology. Every man and woman among them preaches in their own way, always individual, always incarnate.

The liveliness of the lay fraternities is very often staggering. It can sometimes be offset against the challenges imposed by the regimes or the mindsets of the societies in which they thrive. In Vietnam, for instance, when the communist regime hunted down all the friars, the layfolk took over. Bearing witness to the Gospel, taking up Dominic's tradition, they have expanded with courage and patience wherever it was possible. Today they number near on one hundred thousand. In the United States, it is in the very heart of the penal system that inmates have learned to become lay Dominicans within fraternities inspired by Blessed Jean-Joseph Lataste. Prisoners, they preach in prison. Through their witness they proclaim the Kingdom in those places of captivity far beyond their own confinement. So many other examples of evangelizing mission spring to mind, such as attendance in prisons, training of laypeople, escorting the young, visiting the sick. Other laypeople, missionary disciples – these too. Of all the Order's members, its laity is, incidentally, in the vanguard for taking stock of the 'unchurching' common to many societies. And their own experience is essential to enable the Order to best take up the current challenges to evangelization – not least by encouraging laypeople in their capacity to serve as its advocates.

And there exist a host of other forms of association, both ancient and modern, bound up with the Order. Indeed, the diversity of commitments within the Dominican family is potentially limitless. Alongside the sisters, collaborating with them, sizeable 'associated secular' groups share in the distinctive charism of one congregation or another. The International Dominican Youth Movement and Dominican Volunteers International rub shoulders with groups devoted to the prayer and preaching of the Rosary, that central tradition of preaching. Neither can I overlook the members of secular institutes who lead a consecrated life, in the canonical sense, without wishing to do so in community. There are 150 of them in the world. They carry the intuition of the secular life given entirely to God in absolute discretion. To be the leaven in the dough: yet another precious image for our times!

More than 250 diocesan priests belong to the sacerdotal fraternities that the Order contains. They are secular, incardinated (permanently enlisted) in a diocese, and make this choice after their ordination, with their bishop's consent. They aim to pursue their proper vocation as parish priests while at the same time connected with the school of Dominic, exhibiting the meaning of their priestly ministry on a basis of contemplation, study and fraternal communion. They wish to centre their pastoral work on the proclamation of God's Kingdom. These priests commit to the perspective of preaching. Owing to their status, they make no vow of obedience, but promise to contribute to the Preachers' mission by acting within the Master's oversight. Seeking, like the rest of the family, to advance their respective vocations, they afford to them the entire lesson of what makes up the reality of a diocesan church, its needs, its difficulties, its joys. And this contribution is crucial, to the friars in particular.

We like to enumerate the friars, nuns, sisters, all of the religious. Very well, but in order to grasp the full challenge of evangelization today, the Order must particularly learn to reckon with the Dominican laity. The Dominican family must allow itself to be constantly remodelled through fusion between the intuitions of faith and the imperatives of communion: here lies the guarantee of evangelization renewed. For too long, its transmission has proceeded from the clerical pole, at the risk that the experience of life and belief that stems from it should block out the other experiences. Today, an Order such as ours feels a growing awareness that the mission calls for everyone's involvement. In the terms of its origins, it necessarily finds a form of responsibility. Unity, both in a common adventure of preaching and in a common apostolic responsibility, is crucial. All the more so since the lay component of the Order takes on a great topicality for the Church, keen as it is to revive the evangelizing zeal in its contents and its methods.

Wishing to fulfil their baptism by following in Dominic's footsteps, Dominican lay members help both to inform, nurture and enliven the lay vocation in the Church, and to consolidate it in the new demographic but also cultural and ecclesial context that is ours. Preaching needs their commitment, their say and their experience of faith for the same reason as those of the Church's sisters and brothers. Giving them their full place within the Dominican family is a duty for all the members of that family. Going beyond the original complicity, we must devise more viable pathways of synergy, ever more fraternal and actual links of mutual respect and effective collaboration.

A layperson working in a secularized professional world does not face the same problems of faith as a nun who lives in a thirteenth-century convent where bells ring at all hours and rites and rhythms summon to prayer. An observant couple bring to our faith's common welfare their own experience that no insider priest can contribute. Take my concern for the duty to educate children, although I have no children, bring none up, and know at best those of friends and relations. To feel such worries about children of one's own is certainly a different matter. If I want to include family realities in my understanding of faith, as a man of the cloth I must absorb the faith experience of families who happen to be secular – and furthermore, diverse.

So it falls to the Order to structure itself in a reciprocal way. There is a long way to go, but the progress is patent and joyful. To wit, the Dominican Youth Movement and the initiatives taken by various of its groups. Preaching also needs, today, perhaps more than ever, the Christian experience of the young. It needs to pay heed to the specific quality of their life experience, their way of establishing new forms of relations by means of social networks, the hopes and fears the future inspires in their minds, their dreams for a world where they will have their place. Like families, young Catholics are not just the recipients of pastoral ministry. They have their own wealth of experience to offer to the actual work of evangelization, and the Dominican mission needs them.

It is through synergy among all the conditions of life that constitute the Church that the Dominican family can respond most fully to what Paul wrote in his own time to his travelling companion: 'Do the work of preaching the gospel; fulfil the service asked of you'

(2 Tim. 4: 5). So will it be the true heir to the 'holy preaching' of its beginnings.

Move further towards an 'evangelizing' Church

It is not in the power of figures and structures to sum up the innermost mystery of our communion. The Order numbers more lay members than religious, more sisters than friars, and more friars than nuns – who are nevertheless our elder sisters. The numbers do not tell everything. This diversity is the reason why the blossoming of the Dominican spirit and the forwarding of the Dominican family constitute one and the same reality.

The issue is to make it clear that laypeople perform their baptismal vocation in different fashions. Such insights were displayed at the end of the twentieth century by a number of charismatic Catholic groupings, and the pontificate of St John Paul II saw the appearance of what have been called the 'new ecclesial families'. Both of these represent an important moment in the history of Christianity. It is certainly right to see to it that this impulse not confine itself to sentiment or emotion: not for nothing does our tradition insist on the intelligence of faith. But it is equally essential for the Church, in its institutional capacity, to take account of this revival.

For us, it has been eight centuries since Dominic opened a similar path. Hence, what will pose a challenge for the Church in the years to come, and one for all to confront, is already a key topic for the Dominican family, because its whole essence from the start is at stake. The Order, with its many centuries of experience in the service of evangelization, is bound to be concerned by the sea change that will see the Church display a very different face from that of an institution dominated by consecrated men. This is why the overly clerical ways that clergy sometimes have of declaring themselves 'pro-laity' must be flushed out. So powerful is this tendency that it has managed to clericalize some laypeople, which is to say to crystallize false hierarchies within the Church rather than dissolving them. On the contrary, the matter at stake is resolutely to promote evangelizing Christian communities, and to that end laypeople, for their own part, must assume their full place, their role and their function. Not because the clergy so decree it, but because we have, all of us, come to realize that such must be the Church of Jesus Christ.

This is not to say that preaching carries a uniform meaning for all, and that all should have access to delivering the sermon during the celebration of the eucharist. Those are secondary questions that too often arise out of a misunderstanding of true equality and an egalitarianism corrosive of differences. Our diversity must, on the contrary, bring God's plenty to our proclaiming of the Gospel. Rather than blurring distinctions, what matters is that we work together to see that the countless experiences of faith, each in its irreducible core, should engender a common preaching of the Kingdom.

On the morrow of the work to which Pope Francis has called us following the synod on the New Evangelization for the Transmission of the Christian Faith, the family stands out as the very highest of priorities. This event in the life of the Church has urged upon us a fresh awareness of the fact that the family is good news for the life of the world. That it is so with its joys, its frailties and its failures. That each and everybody learns there that they are welcomed into humankind by others, that it is the focal heart of becoming father or mother, son or daughter, brother or sister. Lay members of the Order must see to it that each of these facts informs the preaching of all.

Likewise, the time is right to ponder how, given their complementary nature, the common preaching would benefit from a growth in sacerdotal fraternities. Such a development would undoubtedly invite the brothers to be more mobile and more itinerant. It would push them to respond better to the needs of the ecclesial communities. It would make them more aware of other calls. Many Dominican communities are already in charge of parishes where splendid ventures in evangelization are going on. These put to work the distinctive charism of the Order, notably in animating the joy of the community, its liking for training, the grounding in prayer and a missionary desire to reach out past gateways and frontiers. Today as in the days of its foundation, while so many people do not go to church, or go no longer, especially in the old Europe, the Order must offer its specific contribution to the edification of the Church, a Church that makes itself familiar to all, and the friend of all. Taking up the challenge of fraternity that it sets itself, and rich in its diversity, the Order desires to make this contribution by and for its love of the Church. A 'family of preaching' in the service of the evangelizing Church.

The original freedom that constitutes the most precious legacy of Saint Dominic is to be able to say: 'Let us go further!' This love must impel the Order to make itself available, to renew its foundation, to make its presence felt in places where the pastoral ministry proves less rewarding than in its traditional settings. This same love must urge it to set foot outside the circles of the faithful in order to open a dialogue, even if it seems difficult, with cultures and thinking that seem far removed from Christianity. In some places, love of the Church could even consist in not seeking to fill every gap in the clerical organization chart of pastoral services, in order to open the life of those communities wider to the lay members' own creativity, and to give them charge of evangelizing. Braving the freedom to cast off our own certainties or comforts and find other fields to harvest, other Galilees where Christ precedes us – this is the living understanding of our tradition.

Sustaining discipleship

During our long existence, we have certainly known periods of reform, and diverse trends, but there has always been a single Order. Over the years, friars have laid different stresses, saying that we must pray in this way rather than another, that the rules must be observed more strictly or less, that this or that apostolic, educational or intellectual pathway must be taken. Change does not come easily to an institution, but all those proposals were debated, and many of them adopted, in so far as they might serve the common good. The major risk of U-turns, awakenings and renaissances is that, if this apostolic criterion is overlooked, one ends up restored to oneself, rather than driven with greater fervour to encounter humanity in the haunting concern that proclaiming the Word should achieve this. To this end, the shared responsibility in the unity of preaching and the community of witness has to be constant.

There has always been one single Order because we are preachers in quest of a single preaching, which is Christ's. That is what Dominic wanted. Founder though he was, he desired to efface himself so that the Order be organized around this simple goal – an Order based upon the selfsame impulse, an Order marshalled solely for the sake of evangelization, and requesting all to be similarly self-effacing behind the common aim. Accordingly, all had to learn long ago, and must learn to this day, that the essential issue centres, not on the relevance of their own insights, but rather on their response to the call to embark, along with others, on proclaiming the promise of the Kingdom – and doing so in and for the Church.

Thus since the Preachers' beginnings, our life has been ruled by this essential vision of Saint Dominic. Our unity is in bearing witness, that is, in acquitting ourselves, through our diverse communities, of the unique mission of preaching in the name of Christ's unique mission towards building the unique Church (Eph. 2 and 4). Indeed, in the Church, the one and original mission is that of Christ, himself sent first by the Father to lead us to Him in the Spirit and to assign us as He proclaimed: 'As you sent me into the world, I have sent them into the world' (John 17: 1–26, 18,

23), which is why communion in this same Spirit lies at the heart of the Order's holy preaching.

We strive ceaselessly to practise this truth, which is not always easily done, it must be said. Our good fortune, and what saves us in a sense, is that we first believe in the commitment to fraternity. It displays itself, and always finds its pathways, for as long as diversity prevails and is serenely accepted. This is the message issued by the consecrated life in community to social and secular life: a kind of reminder that standing together is possible. In fact a present and actualized reminder, in the double sense of reality and offering, that communion is what it is.

This requires discarding bipolar views of the religious life. Often it is conceived of, and thereby divided into, two aspects. It seems to be private because the religious make vows, assemble and pray within their communities, which presupposes a contemplative enclosure that sets them apart from the world. It looks public because the religious teach, preach, perform good works, develop solidarities outside their communities, which presupposes an active connection that joins them to the world. But in asking the pope that his brothers be called 'preachers', Saint Dominic did not invite that distinction. He wanted the unity of their religious life to stem from their preaching. They must 'be' preachers. He wanted them to be 'brothers consecrated to the Word' in such a way as to combine their consecrated life and their work of evangelization into a single preaching.

This is the very thing that Jesus wanted when announcing the Good News: he set up an itinerant brotherhood until a 'new family' should emerge with the announcement of the Resurrection made to Mary Magdalene: 'Go to the brothers, and tell them' (John 20: 17). The dispatch of the evangelical mission in the footsteps of Jesus's mission is a call to live this same dynamic of progress towards communion. In the image of this first community of the friends of Jesus, this dynamic is, for us Preachers, our consecration. Our commitments or observances signify first that there is this seed of fraternity in the humanity of men and women. And that it is possible to try to cultivate it.

Thus, in the Dominican family the founders, creators and bearers of projects cannot and must not deem themselves more important than Dominic and his original self-effacement. This is not a matter of replacing the variety of faces with the same face reduplicated; it entails bringing to mind that Dominic effaced himself in order to signal that what matters is the preaching of Christ alone, who mysteriously precedes us wherever we plan to go. The reason why the Order has lasted for eight centuries is precisely the self-effacement required in order to make room for Christ's mission at the heart of the Church. The 'passion' of the disciple must be to see the tent of the Covenant, the friendship of God with humans, built in and by Jesus Christ, spread ever further, out to the ends of the earth. Eventually, we are not an Order of founders but an Order of disciples.

Speaking

The diversity of cultures has always been the hallmark of the Order. It is part and parcel today of its daily life. Within it work brothers and sisters who – and in numbers – outshine their national identities and cultural histories, whereas in the natural way of things those features might have made all dialogue difficult. A Levantine brother whose parents were forced out of their homeland by the advance of Islamic State, and an African brother whose grandmother is a Muslim, can thus exchange their contrasting views of Islam as they build up a living community. African or Asian brothers who hail from traditionally hostile ethnicities can conduct the very same evangelizing project. European brothers can testify that brotherly communion is not impossible in disadvantaged neighbourhoods where immigrations clash. In 1916, for the seven hundredth anniversary of the Order the jubilee celebrations gave rise to a General Chapter. In the midst of the Great War, brothers who came from countries at war in the trenches found themselves gathered around the same table, debating together in the name of preaching the Gospel. Is a finer anniversary imaginable of an Order dedicated to proclaiming the Good News of the Kingdom?

In the manner of the global interfusion that we are seeing, the consecrated life is taking a more and more international and cross-cultural turn. If only on the basis of their life choice, the brothers and sisters are summoned to transform this basic fact into a charism. The world of today is in great need of their witness in order to learn afresh that its future lies not in the juxtaposition and confrontation of identities foreign to one another, but rather in a symphony wherein each person carries the other in what they bring to all.

It might be possible, by the way, to confuse the Order with a multinational company with its headquarters in Rome and subsidiaries scattered worldwide. That is not the case: Dominicanism is no more a brand than the Dominican family issues franchises. Instead, we like to say that we are a communion of communities in which the principle of subsidiarity is fundamental and makes it possible to strengthen the autonomy of each 'base unit': communities within the province, provinces within the Order, all of them in the context of proclaiming a single living Word. On this condition, in cross-culturalism the light of unity, its origin and end, may be seen to shine. Autonomy is always 'connected', arising from creative unity and returning to a unity recapitulated. Its pathway, like its secret in the making, is fraternity.

The Order has been readily credited with the invention of democracy. That is not mistaken, but nor is it valid if this word denotes the regime invoked in political modernity. Unity among Preachers does not involve a winning majority and a losing opposition with an outcome measured in figures. It requires that each component of the whole be integrated into a more global agenda of which it is neither the owner nor the judge. That is why the chapters are vital. The life of the communities, the mission plans of the provinces, any number of evangelizing projects are raised there for common consideration, so that the brothers may assess them together, identify their urgencies or priorities, plan new foundations and send brothers there. Despite the inevitable biases and oppositions, what prevails is the common desire for our unity in one and the same apostolic discourse. Owing to this pursuit, the chapter represents that moment when the brothers manage to confirm the Order anew.

In chapter, where everyone's concerns are tabled for debate by everyone, each of those attending must be able to express not just their view, but the ground on which it is held, confident that they will be heard out, free of preconceptions. Only an exchange conducted in mutual trust can generate the option that enjoys the greatest unanimity and will gather the widest support. As ever, the objective is to establish a communion respectful of diversity. That is not always easy, nor always efficient, in the short run at least, but learning to become free together remains a splendid aspiration.

Hence our system, democratic as it is, does not match the model that prevails in contemporary liberal societies. It does not involve the idea that unity is final, but perceives it as a starting point. Its stated aim is not to thrash out opinions, but to rally convictions in a tireless democratic quest for unity. Such a dynamic supposes the culture of dialogue that the brothers of a given community or province set out to cultivate as the days go by, and this in the simplest way, which is talking to each other. Is the election of a new provincial in the offing? The brothers talk. The drafting of the minutes of chapter must not be delayed? The brothers talk. The constitutions, the rules of living, of the Order need adjusting? The brothers talk. Each time, the aim is to identify what the body is ready to accept, what will enlist the full support of all, whichever way they may have voted.

The margin is wide that enables people to speak their mind without disrespect to the other. The true breach of human dignity consists in reducing the word that is not my own to a mere opinion void of meaning or value. Preventing this abuse is never ruled out, once it is acknowledged that nobody triumphs or gives in by admitting that the 'we' comes first. Being with us all means that all stand together with all, and that all collect the stake. What stake? Communion, fragile at times, always contagious. In medical philosophy, we say that there is no lesser pain. The same goes for the good. The Order lives by the spreading within it of the Word and of speech.

Self-effacement

The foremost risk with preaching is pride. A major temptation is to believe that to preach you need to be a prophet. Now no one can declare themselves as such – a claim that any sensible person will always be astonished to find made about them. We bestow the description of prophet only on someone who utters a word acknowledgeable and acknowledged as coming from another than ourselves. It is likewise a great temptation to believe that to speak of the Word of God amounts to laying down a moral rule. Morality does not tell all about the mystery of faith. And if grace surpasses the law, the same must go for proclaiming the Gospel.

When a man sets out to speak of God, or in the name of God, he risks putting God to use to buttress his own words. Whereas the Preacher's adventure is inspiring in a different way: Christ agrees to resort to my human words to make His own – divine – Word heard. The stake in preaching is to learn to be quiet so as to make Him heard: Him. As to moralizing, you would be left having to explain about Saint Paul spending his time, in his early life, doing damage to Christians. Or about the triple betrayal of Saint Peter, our first pope. It would remain to pay proper attention to the fact that the advent of God's mercy in Jesus His Son transfigures the world and saves it, because this mysterious gift engenders everybody anew, reborn and made new. In short, it must be said that at the heart of moral or ritual prescriptions lies this mystery of a God who comes to make an alliance with humanity such that it should have life, and life in abundance. That mystery calls for silence.

Quite apart from the humility evoked by the saints, at the very least there persists the call to remember that He Himself said: 'I would like You to keep them in my word. This I ask of You. Stay in my word', as recorded in various verses of John's Gospel. Now, we think we know His Word by reason of having heard, read and studied it. But to stay with the word of another asks us, not to claim to know it once and for all, or that we possess it, but to go on wanting to be surprised by it. How is it, then, with the Word of God? When you are drafting a sermon, the greatest delight is to discover a word, a train of thought, a reference hitherto gone unnoticed. Like a footnote, perhaps, but as good as a flash of light. A 'next to nothing' that changes everything.

How hard it is to accept that there is no need to strike attitudes to be worthy of God! It is He who, through His grace, adjusts us to Him. It is He who, so as to get talking to us, lowers himself to our level. It is He who has it in Him to be human – and who for this reason did not wish to 'count equality with God something to be grasped' – and became 'in every way like a human being' (Phil. 2: 6–11). When one adopts this position, to take up the Word on God's behalf is always risky, but what a joy to know him so close!

In this sense are we disciples for ever. Nobody will ever be able to claim to possess the Gospel. We must always discover that we are the destination of the Word that we carry. It also wants to speak to me. The Preacher's good fortune is that at the very heart of what he does, the Word returns to him in other wise than he would have believed. Such is the highest gift extended to the Dominican.

Observing the invisible

No doubt it is in this surprise resumed, in this unapparent little that overturns the whole of the visible, in this listening to the underside of the world, that the first reason for the Order's longevity has to be seen. Because people pray there, study there, preach there. Because the tradition of the Order is great, very great. But also and above all because each and everybody has their place there and finds in the great observances devised by Dominic a complete guide to life, open to whoever will open themself likewise to the truth, within their own means, each to their measure, no more and no less.

We take pride, for example, in laying claim as a brother to Thomas Aquinas, but not all brothers are Thomas Aquinas. When I was a young student, at the very start of the 1980s, to bring home to us the importance of theological thought, our teachers would stress key figures like Marie-Dominique Chenu and Yves Congar. Through their authoritative works, both had profoundly influenced the proceedings of the Second Vatican Council. Yet, that was just two friars out of the five hundred that made up the province of France. That is why the preaching of them all, its joys and hardships, held such importance in the eyes of these spokespersons of the Order. They knew their place and were certainly not unaware of their own shortcomings. No matter how great their humility, they acted this way out of realism.

Seeking to live through past glories is another means of missing the call addressed personally to us. We go to such great lengths to elude that tipping point where it suffices to learn to achieve what we are meant for, what we are capable of – and what renders us useless servants. To be what one is among the many, no more and no less; not to exist in and for oneself but with and through one's fellows. It is through the observance of fraternity that one must grasp the meaning of being brothers in diversity, without taking the easy way of choosing to be this one's brother, but not that one's. Fraternity is not for you to decide, but to receive. It is in the image of God, who likewise is not to be manufactured. He too has to be let inside so as to truly become His son or daughter.

Neither is the truth a mental construct. It already exists. It has both a name and a face, that of Christ. Which again determines against expectation the observance of study within the Order. To study consists in knowing better and in better understanding the revelation of Christ in order to expound, articulate and share it. Those who devote themselves to its pursuit find themselves like Moses before the Burning Bush (Exod. 3: 1–6). He sees the bush on fire, fails to understand why it burns but is not consumed, thinks that he must come closer, walks around the blaze, and just as he thinks he is close enough for it to scorch him, a voice tells him that he has forgotten to take off his sandals, for the ground he is standing on is holy. Study is like that: entering contemplative research as one ventures into a holy place. Brush up against the truth, and it evades your grasp. It escapes you because it is not a thing but a Person. A Person you cannot master.

The letting-go of self runs in parallel in preaching. You think to advance human words that you have pondered, worked on and rehearsed. But the finest of experiences comes when the Word itself takes hold of you, wrecking the dykes you have built with its impact. Those you addressed come and thank you for words you do not recall having spoken. And probably they heard them when you did not say them. It is they, your listeners, who speak to you then on behalf of Him about whom you spoke to them in the belief that you knew what you were going to say. Through them He makes you hear something new about Himself.

Whatever you may do, whatever you say, never will you know what will matter most in order for the Gospel to express God's friendship for humankind. Deep down, you do not know much except that you want to speak about Him. And it is indeed He who is there, and who calls for unity: 'that they may be one' (John 17: 1–11). This prayer of Jesus's is, deep down, the heart and bedrock of the Order's prayer. It is in the night's meditation of Dominic and in his intercession, in the nuns' contemplation, in the praying of the brothers and sisters and lay members. It works tirelessly to bring the promised communion and so that all may find their place and commit there. Contemplative prayer, study and meditation on the Holy Word, the surprise of fraternity, the burning desire that the Name of Jesus Christ should become the name of the friend of the greatest number: those are our observances, each one of which invites self-dispossession for the Gospel's sake.

A taste for silence

The more that our time mistrusts faith, the more it trusts in beliefs. The more it renounces authority and transmission, the passing on of custom and tradition, the more it embraces submission and quick returns. Spiritualities, methods and gurus thrive, as in the time of Dominic. What is true of the hardship zones of the South is also true of the areas of affluence in the North. And sometimes, unbearably, in the very heart of the Church. Now the Order was, to an extent, founded so as to resist this temptation of methods and masters. It responded and continues to respond to them through the intimate bond that it fosters with the silence said to be 'the father of Preachers'.

To be silent: would that not be a paradoxical vow for preachers? Quite the reverse: herein lies preaching's major challenge. Its purpose is not that the hearer should retain what is put to them, should make themself a rule out of what they are told and have it stick in their mind, but rather that they encounter Him who is heralded. In the heart of all preaching lies that key moment when one must fall silent, withdraw and let Jesus tread discreetly close in the silence.

The preacher proclaims to the now that there is Good News. He testifies that the mystery of Revelation lights up the present of History as it has lighted and will light its every moment. But he proclaims it to real people, concrete flesh-and-blood individuals, in their own right. He wants them to understand that he is speaking to them about someone infinitely closer and more familiar than he himself, the preacher, will ever be able to be. The ultimate ambition of the preacher is to leave his hearers in conversation with Him whose very contemplation leaves him speechless.

That is how people will discover Him who, alone, sides once and for all with them, to the very depths of their life, its joys and its pains intermingled. It is in dialogue with Him that they will discover their own capacity for discernment and moral decision, for communion and goodness. It is Christ who, in the Spirit, will 'set them free' through truth (John 8: 32). The preacher must be silent so as to listen. So as to efface themself behind Jesus's Word. To gauge to what extent their own human words prove muted to echo His with justice. So that they may be able to murmur to the person before them, through a relation of friendship, this confidence: 'He wants to speak to you,' in the way of Mary when she tells the servants at Cana to do whatever He will ask. Preaching is this: nothing from the preacher, everything from Him.

Lengthy or brief matters little. Silence grounds the mystery as it prevails after communion, as must happen in confession and in the sermon. I can concentrate for as long as I may, nothing will change if I keep to rational calculation. What matters is for the silence to brim with the joy of an encounter. That I come face to face with Him, who comes to me as a friend and as a brother. The aim is for me to be silent, in order to listen and truly to hear the questions that come to me, without seeking to answer them before I have understood where they lead me, towards whom they are leading me. To be silent and listen together to the still small voice of God 'in the sound of sheer silence' (1 Kings 19: 12).

Short of which, there is a risk of straying into spiritualist habits. It is easy to lapse into subjectivism, to fancy oneself a mystagogue or initiate, to concoct for oneself a total and definitive formula of life. So many impostors reinvent themselves as emancipated figures in order to exercise a tyranny over minds. The desire for domination that drives them comes to fill the voids in isolated individuals trapped in their own imagination and liable to be gullible, often more aware of their frailties and injuries than of their true capacities. This is amplified by the current tendency to perceive the fact of existence as a continual misfortune. In its wake comes the illusion of a spiritual solution that, as if by magic, will solve all problems.

Indeed, each one of us now and then bears the full burden of being alive, and may verge on a state of extreme insecurity, sometimes even of utter vulnerability. Once you would be offered amulets and charms to ward off ill-fortune; today it is recipes for making good choices, so as to alleviate the strains of the uncertain and to instil self-confidence. Before our eyes, a host of advisers and coaches of all stripes have proliferated, who claim to have answers for everything. You don't know what to do about your children, your job, the ups and downs of your love life, the latest fashions, the new technologies, persistent addictions, what book to read, what diet to follow, what clothes to wear? Here's the thing! You are told, given guidance, prescribed. Faced with the unlikely scale of your existence, you are daunted by your own uncertainty? Here are certainties and guarantees! Here's what will silence the insomnia of uncertainty, fruitful though it is.

By comparison with the mystical life in which all of us struggle to put into words what we perceive as being transcendental, the promise of these professors of solutions is to make God accessible in a few lessons, which amounts to reifying Him and turning Him into a consumer good. And in seeking in too hasty or too authoritarian a way to issue reassurances about God, you finish by destroying yourself from within and destroying the others around you. Now while churches are no more immune to this risk than are other human communities, it is their singular duty to avert it.

The Gospel teaches us better than any other doctrine. Human life is both simple and difficult. It contains tragedies and beauties. It takes on sorrows and joys. Nothing in it is reducible to a system of resolves, even a spiritual system. The issue and the stuff of human life is not to identify problems and define solutions, but to pursue the way from difficulty past to difficulty new. Existence is not linear. In the midst of it, the moments alternate when the notes ring true or ring false, instants when one feels unified or when one feels torn. Its course may seem chaotic, but there is no other path on which to greet Him who comes to walk beside us. One learns to look to the future with confidence by living out the mystery of Salvation brought, once and for all, by the Cross. The surprises in store on such a journey leave no room for the gurus who want to bend them into algorithms. A characteristic of the Order is that properly speaking there neither is nor could be a 'Dominican method', other than that of learning to live as brothers, to stay in the Word in friendship with the world. We Preachers know only how to be the disciples of that friend of the encounter who is Jesus.

Embarking on friendship with God

In the North as in the South, in all countries and regardless of the culture of the place, a great need is being expressed to be heard and accompanied in the flow both of life and of faith, and sometimes to be consoled for too hard a life. Many brothers and sisters devote the bulk of their time to this. For them it is not simply a matter of holding a fraternal and well-meaning conversation, but of standing together, with the other whom they receive, and listening to a Word that is addressed to each and that no one is confined by. Such are the marks of these free partnerships.

Always, we are tempted to dwell on our own limitations. 'Leave me, I'm dying,' says the man. 'No, you're not,' we are tempted to reply, as if to plug the gap that split us in our turn. And yet we do know, or we sense, that in the presence of a person who sees their end approaching, a more honest emblem of friendship is to sit at their side and be silent. To listen: God's friendship stands out as the surest path to facing up fearlessly to questionings, the more so in cases where the recipes fail, whether true or false.

To whoever feels too empty or too full, one might reckon to offer ready-made solutions, but they would be lies. Furthermore, the experience of listening shows that to go to the limits of another's anxiety is easier than grasping the beginnings of one's own. In that respect the venture of preaching overlaps with the narrow and demanding path of conversion, because it calls for moving off-centre from oneself, for daring to believe that in sharing the hearing of the Word with others, some day at last each will dare to let that Word console them. Upon this path everyone finds themselves invited to accept the person they are without either retreating into a fixed identity or locking themselves in crushing loneliness. Upon this path, each traveller finds themself invited to discover and accept the subject that they are, without either taking refuge in a set identity or walling themself into a crushing solitude. Along this path, one learns to rejoice that the world is not reducible to dualist readings – pure and impure, licit and forbidden, like and unlike, those who comfort and those who thwart me.

Somewhere along this path one bumps into Dominic. Tradition informs us that one day a friar, Bertrand de Garrigues, one of his first companions, came to visit him. During the conversation, Bertrand began to weep as he detailed his personal failings and shortcomings. Dominic listened to him before asking him to weep no more over his own sins, but rather to shed his tears over others'. This is the magnificent reply that every preacher shoulders who is anxious for his eternal future: you are not wrong to bewail your sins, but as long as the quest for consolation does not avail for each and every man and woman – for all the world – there is still a long road to travel before you taste that deep joy of being at one with all of humanity in greeting the same promise of salvation. And living it through! 'Your time will come, no doubt,' but in the meantime, within this realm of the inconsolable dwells the spur of evangelization, that other name of preaching.

He it is, the Unconsoled, invisible for whoever will not or cannot see him, silent for whoever will not or cannot hear him, who stands at the heart of the most modest, the tiniest reality. The danger for the life of the Order, for the consecrated life, for the life of the Church, would be to conceive of reality as deriving from the extraordinary, the exotic, the sensational. Hence, less than ever must Preachers glorify places that are counted as exemplary. The witness of brothers and sisters confronted with especially difficult apostolic situations is to me a vital oxygen. But they themselves instruct me that preaching must be done, quite simply, where people hunger and thirst for the Kingdom.

The friendship of God is commonplace in so far as, in order for us to grasp it, know it, live it, God himself wished to make himself ordinary. To observe the Dominican life is to learn to see this secret that lies at the heart of the world – the ordinary world. To hear the footsteps of Him who comes into the underside of the world.

4

ENCOUNTERING THE WORLD

Seized by the real

To wander and beg our way towards the Kingdom –
that is the single roadmap Saint Dominic left us. It is
the sole destination that all paths can lead to, once we
pursue to the end the one we adopt and acknowledge
as our own, hard as it sometimes is to make out its
luminous conclusion. The path that humanity is
following today cannot be unblessed with, and still
less devoid of this light, be it as fragile as dawn's. Yet
what is dismaying is the tracts of darkness that are
gathering there.

The Master of the Order is a pilgrim among pilgrims.
But his mission also requires that he should set out
to meet the diverse communities that constitute the
Dominican family over the five continents, and that –
each from its unique starting point – are embarked on
the same transition. So I have had occasion to travel
the length and breadth of this vast world from Rome,
and to cover its many and seemingly infinite facets.

That is a privilege, a marvel and a joy. It is also an ordeal for the depths that prove to neighbour the wealthy heights.

I would like to linger on the fine advances I catch glimpses of, and which manifest the infinite creativity that God grants so that some day all may be one. But I cannot do so without also mentioning the undersides, which are just as many rebuffs for the sense of humanity. It is they that strike me, so much do they loom up and multiply. I see all too many fractures and closures, sufferings and dangers. These crunch points of temptation that I come across everywhere are known as identity inflation, political indifference and educational disaffection. They all give me grounds for deep disquiet as regards the destructive powers of globalization.

I see the spread of identity politics, be it national, cultural or religious, but also by opinion or generation, most often with the sole aim of rewriting history around its narrator, shutting out the other and spreading violence. This trend appears all the more scandalous to me when confessional beliefs are co-opted to arm or counter-arm this latent civil war on a global scale. This brand of radicalism is no longer of the eschatological variety that prevailed in Dominic's days, but its totalitarian translation into the mania to pre-decide who one is, predesignate friend and foe, and predetermine the frontier. In other words to restrict solidarity to a common cause chosen in one's own image so as the better to dominate it, rather than receiving it as an invitation to make oneself at home elsewhere. This prospect alarms me.

I see the indifference to alienation growing. The small number of those who have everything consider that they can continue to develop according to their own logic in utter contempt and disregard for the great mass who have nothing. The rich who are richer and richer deliberately crush the poor who are poorer and poorer. And the powerful, who believe that they can just shrug off the marginalized. It is precisely the unflappable banality of this verdict on the modern city, depoliticized under the impact of accepted injustices, that has grown intolerable to me.

I see the spread of disaffection towards the young and not so young who all over the world have no means of access to education. There is talk of fighting illiteracy; there is no talk of how many illiterate or uncultured people are involved. In too many places, school has become a ruthless sorting ground, and study beyond the elementary comes at a financial and human price impossible to afford. The instantaneous rule of mass communication, with its successive images of a life that must nevertheless learn to 'last', to which children are subjected at an ever younger age, erodes the protracted patience for acquiring knowledge without which there is no free, liberated and autonomous subject. Not only does the legacy that we are preparing to leave them come with a heavy debit side, but also they must get by without the keys to understand the disaster and respond to it. We fate them for a difficult future, yet fail to prepare them to be agents equipped to ground their opinions in critical analysis. This causes me great concern.

There are just as many reasons to be jealous of the Dominican tradition and to pass it on in the way that it has come to us since its foundation. In the Order, we distrust reductions of identity, for they would forbid its very existence. In the Order we are proud of the democratic practices which, ever since foundation, have asked of us, in the name of the common good, always to seek the utmost unanimity, affording to each the possibility of taking part in the process. In the Order we cherish study as a fundamental discipline towards the mission of preaching. No doubt this tradition makes us particularly aware of what is lacking in the world today. There is no room for triumphalism here, but to the contrary the present viewed through the features of humanity's worsening misfortune rekindles the desire to share our centuries of insight and experience.

Alerting against evil

As proof that the decision for God is always possible, even while the sombre page of the Inquisition was being written another page opened, this time a shining one, for its bearing on the emergence of human rights.

In 1510 the Preachers arrived on the island of Hispaniola, at a time when the dominant culture viewed it as self-evident that the 'Indians' should be subject to the rule of the Europeans and exploited for the sake of their expansion and enrichment. Our brothers were not free from that bias, but soon found themselves deeply grieved by the sad spectacle laid before their eyes. They realized that such a doctrine was not to be accepted, and dared to throw public doubt on the obvious fact – to put the stifled question concerning the unity of humankind.

These friars, among them Pedro de Córdoba and Antonio de Montesinos, hailed from the University of Salamanca. Very well schooled in philosophy as in theology, it was their custom to pray and to study the Word together so as to ground their shared fraternity and preaching. It was on the strength of this background that they found themselves acting as pastors in so outlandish and upsetting a context. So it was that during the Advent of 1511, on 21 December, as they read the liturgical texts, they realized that they were seeing clues to the present: 'A voice cries, "Prepare in the desert a way for Yahweh"' (Isa. 40: 3), echoed by John the Baptist: 'I am the voice of one that cries in the desert' (John 1: 23).

The Preachers decided to inform the lords and masters of colonization, their fellow countrymen, that they could not in good conscience voice their will to power by reducing to servitude the inhabitants of a land in which they were only guests, and to which, incidentally, no one could claim valid ownership. In the name of them all, Montesinos spoke out to alert them to that equal dignity of all human beings that they were infringing, but also to the jeopardy they incurred to their own salvation. 'These men, these Indians, are they not men for you?' He was not appealing to their reason alone, but also to their faith and their humanity. He told them not only that they must do no harm to these small fry, but that they were doing harm to themselves. Montesinos confronted the conquistadors with the inexorable imperative of communion without which life is nothing but death. Are they not men? Are we not all humans, with them?

Yet the friars knew full well the price of such a combat. They made public their concern, sent emissaries to the court of Spain, and took to witness public opinion and the powers of the day. Attempts were made to gag them, to prevent them from leaving again, and to eliminate them. But the brothers continued the mission they had found waiting. They worked with the masters of the School of Salamanca to give their indignation a rational and positive status. The Dominican theologians and jurists who made up the School took heed in their considerations of the witness of these Preachers back from the New World. They developed a 'Law of Peoples' which was to source a true conceptual revolution that had its roots in the Gospel. Today in the United Nations office in Geneva, the big Human Rights room is named, for this reason, after the most eminent among them, Francisco de Vitoria, who in 1532 published *De Indis*, in which he condemned the Spanish conquest as illegitimate and intolerable because it breached the laws on ownership and destroyed the sanctity of the person.

It was the same conviction that brought about the dual conversion of Bartolomé de Las Casas, who upon hearing Antonio de Montesinos preaching asked to be admitted among the Dominicans. During the Valladolid controversy of the mid-sixteenth century it would impel his opposition to any subservience of the Gospel to the logic of the world and its empires. As a true heir to Dominic, Bartolomé was to see himself first of all as a preacher of freedom. Not content to attest to it, he would fight – and successfully – to wring essential reforms of laws and ways of thinking out of the political establishment of his time.

Friars like Pedro de Córdoba, Antonio de Montesinos, Francisco de Vitoria and Bartolomé de Las Casas, ready to open and pave pathways of holy rebellion, are thin on the ground, it might be said, by way of excuse for shirking and inertia. We know nonetheless that there are many contemporary situations that can be read today as theirs were then. As in times past, the dominant present-day cultures would like to forget the fact of their own greed, to turn a blind eye to the number of victims of their ambitions. Today as in the past, philosophers, theologians and pastors must stand up together and confront the unanswered questions raised by the ascendancy of the new Hispaniolas.

Pedro, Antonio, Francisco, Bartolomé and their brothers asserted that it is not possible to preach the Gospel if there is no solidarity of destiny – if my flesh does not become one with the flesh of those who suffer. The Church communion, the Body of Christ, must be wounded by those who suffer and who count for nothing. Down the centuries, the Order, like many others, has been and still is led to enshrine this conviction at the heart of its preaching, starting from the experience and reflection of its sisters and brothers. Today, in memory of Montesinos's sermon and on the occasion of its anniversary, the Dominicans have declared as a priority what they have called the Salamanca Process. It is an ever-present challenge for philosophers, theologians and jurists, along with many others, to call to the common awareness the injustice and dishonesty involved in these intolerable human and social situations that urgently call for the rights both of individuals and of peoples to be revisited again and reviewed.

In order to be present in the field of human rights, we maintain a permanent, if still modest, delegation at the United Nations Organization. I do not wish to overstate our own importance, or that of that assembly, but I am keen for our experience to be heard there, and to become a stakeholder in the global debate around peace, justice and ecology. It is possible to make the Gospel heard there, to 'proclaim the Kingdom' to the nations by, above all, enhancing the voice of the forgotten. The dignity of the world resides in its ability to construct itself by making all welcome. The Order's international reality thus invites us to create a link between the actual solidarities achieved by means of preaching, and the efforts towards establishing a more universal solidarity, a stepping stone towards eschatological communion. That is the whole work of the Gospel within the substance of the human make-up, the emergence of small groups in communion that aspire to be quasi-sacraments of universal friendship.

We are an old Order. We have travelled in the footsteps of the expansion of the European world. We have seen how ambivalent the culture of the West could be, veering between the wonder of discovery and the pretension to hegemony. We have learned how hard it was to correct this ambiguity within ourselves. We have to pay attention to this history. It is the duty of an Order as ancient as ours not to abandon ourselves to amnesia about the past, so as not to give way to blindness to the present.

Within the Dominican family, that episode of 1510 is therefore a constant reminder of how to behave. If we wish to keep up an active dialogue with the alienated cultures without remaining the passive accomplices of the dominant ones, we have to devise updated forms of that same spirit of resistance. A new moral creativity is called for so as to secure for all – individuals and peoples alike – the right to inhabit the world. I do not see how it is possible to speak about the Kingdom if one leaves people by the roadside, if one does not grasp something of their hardship by letting it grasp oneself. It is the Samaritan finding the man by the wayside who inaugurates the communion that the preachers seek (Luke 10: 29–37).

Resisting fatality

In my travels, I have seen too many of those shantytowns, their mud walls, their open sewers, their crossroads where people are left to die. The eyes of this mother trying to feed her child with the pitiful scraps of a sandwich retrieved from the garbage . . . who could remain indifferent to the prospect? Who would not acknowledge it? And yet there is no need to go to the ends of the earth to know its extent. The tragedies and anxieties of today are a vital concern in preaching the Gospel. Not simply urgent but immediate. Not elsewhere but here. Relevant not solely for the visible needy but for every man and woman, for there is no one alive who does not feel the need to be acknowledged in the unique plenitude of love.

The empire of all the riches would like to believe, and to have it believed, that the worlds of poverty are not its underside; that at worst they are its negative print, that by dint of a few more sacrifices to the idols of finance, success and performance this foul spectre would vanish away. But that is false. There will always be an underside of the world. Those on the side of plenty know, though too often they feign not to, that there exists another side, and it is penury. I want to believe that many on the one side are not proud, and are not happy, as they survey how many elsewhere, on the other, are crushed and bereft. Their own underside is the void that they surmise in their own heart, and that no act of charity could ever fill – all the less if intended as munificent and planned. An emptiness, all the same, that can open the path to standing together with a common humanity.

It is with both these sides that God would like to enter into conversation. In the Bible, the Covenant summons and gathers all human beings, in that it acknowledges in each of them, no matter who they may be, the fundamental right always to be able to partake in it and never to be refused it (Isa. 56, Jer. 31). The Covenant carries a risk. It corresponds to the very wager God makes for 'the salvation of many'. But this fundamental right entails a duty, that of saying no to what denies it, of resisting whoever may gainsay it. The right to communion has as its corollary the duty of rebellion.

The widow's mite (Luke 21: 1–4), the paralytic lowered from the roof (Mark 2: 1–12), the two blind men outside Jericho (Matt. 20: 29–34) are at the heart of Jesus's teaching. Their existences seem minimal, but in that alone, they rule out the temptation of idealization, the ridicule of kindness to order, the 'moralic acid' that Nietzsche was right to denounce. Those who count for next to nothing are no worse than those who count for more than a lot. But the simple fact that they should be such as they are is not acceptable. There is here a demand beyond dispute: the table does not belong to the Master if it makes no room, besides the disciples and the women who follow them, for the blind at birth, the insignificant and the sinners. Let all be one, as in the icon of the oneness of the Trinity painted by Andrei Rublev: in proclaiming the Kingdom of God, the Gospel announces His advent not only at the end of times, but also in the present time, and very often as from the underside of the world.

Globalization produces the oppression and the marginalization of shunned identities, of uneducated people, of unprofitable countries, and does so with utter impunity. I believe that it is every person's duty to rebel against this worldwide process of exclusion of the dispossessed, to join them in the fight against what Pope Francis calls a global 'culture of waste'. Each one of the injustices that human beings sink to, and that disfigure them, amounts to another deadening obstacle that they set before themselves. If we want centres of communion to establish themselves, which would amount to as many sacraments revealing what humanity is destined to become, we must start by including those who are shut out from it. This has to start from them, and with them. Let them act with us and for us. To my eyes, that is the absolute priority. That is the lever made to move the world, if it is to rise to the height of its proper dignity.

To be sure, once that essential concern is identified, it is necessary to resist the panic that would have it turn into an ideology. However, to focus on that fear and hold it as a reason not to act would represent an even greater evil. In the same way as would blaming the solitude or the ineffectiveness of the combat for withdrawing from it. I do not ask myself the questions of whether the struggle is futile, or those who join it too few, or whether such a struggle has no end – or rather I would like not to have to ask them in order to answer those who see fit to raise them with me.

It is in the whole world over that the humiliated poor are to be found. In rich countries they are granted allowances according to a system so complicated that they often get it wrong, sometimes swindle it, and find themselves condemned between repeated applications and recurrent insolvency, with their resigned silence bought off by a new recipe for aid. What role does the yardstick of dignity play, in this logic of assistance that is in fact letting fall? The countries hit by hardship are mostly unaware of such support mechanisms, and the descent into extreme poverty knows no end and no return. But for one or another of these nowhere people, assisted or not, the question is the same: to count for something or to count for nothing, to be heard or to go unheard, to be considered as a partner or not. They want to be acknowledged. They are not.

On the underside of the world there are people without whom the world must not accept living. We may well – and indeed we must – build schools, health centres, asylums, or even devise reintegration policies. But the hardest task is not to build a lie by making do with salving the urgency, by numbing the most virulent or the most inflammable social sores, by treating hardship with statistics. The forgotten of the world, lost in the collateral damage of history, are people essential to the human community. If, because they are self-effacing, they go missing, it becomes inhuman.

We are more than a few, in the Order and, in the Church, who share this concern. Many of the faithful – most of them, once outside the zones of abundance – count among those people liable to be pushed around and forgotten. And there are multitudes with no one to speak for them. What happens to them happens to us. I do not feel that I have a particular mission. Faced with this call that signals a priority, I would not be true to myself if I concealed or even played it down. It is this that I have to live out, and that I would like to live more fully, for it is to this, as a Dominican, that I believe myself committed.

How are we to avoid inconsolable wounds, incurable fractures, unforeseeable cataclysms, short of promoting such a joint resistance? We know that humiliation and neglect foment violence. It is true of the peoples stripped of their destiny, yesterday so distant, today so close. It is no less true of the nameless individuals of our own countries, relegated to the margins, 'little people', 'on the rocks', 'down and out', 'out of work', 'no fixed abode', 'on the street', and who also shout their anger. Now all of these, to us, evoke Jesus Christ, who alone, when humiliated, did not turn the violence he suffered back against those who inflicted it. He, the Word, whom they tried to silence, so as to put a stop to His threat to this false order of lies. They sought to take His life so as to preserve their sole franchise on God. He gave His life saying that there is only one possible point of departure towards another future for the world: *Veritas* – Truth – the word that, given their motto, binds the Preachers.

Suffering from being wounded

Human contact grounds a Preacher's programme. In Lille, as the community prepared to celebrate the Nativity, a drunken man threw open a flap of the church door with a noisy clatter, settled down on a bench and heard out my request to quieten down before leaving again with another din. He could return, he knew, as I told him, and so he did the following week. He was what society calls a tramp. He had 'dropped out', lost in alcohol and violence. We were to be friends for many years. When he went missing, I would look for him. When he tried to quit alcohol, I came along to the appointment. When he voiced the wish, I met his wife. His life was hard and I feared for him. One night, he was killed in the street. He came home at last, but only to be buried. His two children were there. In the cemetery, standing by his grave, his ten-year-old son said: 'Now I know where he is.' That is the recognition that is always in store.

It is not up to the Order to possess the aims and skills of the social security arm that it is not. Its only skill is to promote the intuition preached by the friars in so far as they are wounded by the friendship of God and of His people, that their destiny cannot be kept separate from that wound, and that the scarring that derives from it and that they carry lasts for ever. What do we all have in common? The mercy of God. What is mercy? The love that is God. The love that distresses God to the bowels of His Being when He sees His people fallen into slavery. The love through which God wants to free His people and to have it live again. The mercy is that love thanks to which God engenders life again. In that sense it reveals the truth of God: that all can be reborn in His mercy.

That is why the Order, preacher of grace and of mercy, gives so much precedence to the human reality that is the friendship of one another, of some for others. In order for it to preach mercy, it is good for the family of Dominic to be wounded by the conjugation of all the friendships that bind to the upper as also to the underside of the world. But there again, it is a matter of listening both to what this calling says, and to what it does not. The desire for friendship cannot be waved about like an action plan. Still less so if those friendships lie on the underside of the world. There is no social specialization or political agenda here. We are only the preachers of mercy through friendship lived, as it is given, for what it is. A prism enabling everything to be captured and recaptured at that focal point where destinies combine. This is what we should be able to share in the Order so as to vouch for the promise of communion. Yet might this be merely a promise, always eluding whoever ventures close to it? No, God's fidelity is true, and paramount. It means that, first of all, I am trustful. He is already here, who fulfils the promise. And then, yes, I am impatient for us to all be happy to be with Him in this adventure.

Trust deeply felt translates into the patience of friendship. This is how the Gospel invites us to respond to the assortment of systems that claim the power to bring heaven down to earth straight away, and hence grow toxic. How else to understand that Jesus, seeing Zacchaeus in his tree (Luke 19: 1–10), should then go on to his house to find himself among people many of whom are no doubt unconvinced by his teaching? Was he wounded by this? We do not know. What cannot be ignored is that the wound, if wound there was, did not matter.

The right-thinking and the right-believing were, for their part, angry with Him. Because Jesus dined among sinners. Because Jesus overstepped the boundaries. His response did not come with grand speeches. Quietly, patiently, Jesus proclaimed the promise of communion by establishing God's friendship with these people. Now could he say that the Kingdom was at hand. He simply wanted to establish God's friendship with all. An Order that sees itself as Preachers has the task of finding how, as best it can, it can further this freedom of Jesus's.

Taking the plunge

The freedom to see the world in the way that it does matters all the more because in many societies we are seeing a sizeable reorganization. It is not enough to deplore the erosion of the lower-middle classes, the enfeebling of intermediate groups, the discrediting of institutions, or again the expansion of corruption. More than ever, democracy needs to be solidly grounded in an explicit body of thought that rallies the commitment of the greatest number. This is imperative if we are to avoid the risk of populist rulerships that manipulate opinions rather than promoting that capacity for critical thinking that would make each of its members a qualified agent taking their share of responsibility for the common good. In this respect, the Churches' reflection on their structures may help societies to question themselves, in their turn, about their own initiative.

It is too often said, I believe, that the Church has no business in politics. It certainly matters to keep the temporal sphere separate from the spiritual one in order to avoid all confusion. But to distinguish and to differentiate between them is not be reduced to penning up the fact of religion within the precincts of the home, disconnecting it from the global life of each individual and making the social and political dimensions of their existence foreign to them. The lights of the faith, where the subjective has no part to play, must have a right to speak in the public space in order to contribute to the civic debate. It is not entitled to impose its specific convictions, or the laws that govern them. But these convictions are based upon making heard the questions that they ask in the context of the promise that they carry and of the historical time in which it arises. To urge them to silence, and worse still to enforce it, respects neither the human person nor the social instinct. Modern democracy will be strengthened to the extent that the linkage of these two dignities is sustained.

Always, the Church must take the side of humanity and of the human. It follows, *ipso facto*, that it cannot be partisan. It cannot give way to that temptation, neither actively nor passively. But because it bears, in the heart of the world, the sign that the human is communion, it cannot stand apart from the efforts that humans make in common to build an open, enduring and hospitable world. Does not Pope Francis's encyclical *Laudato Sì*, in which he recalls and updates the Church's social doctrine, and whose profundity and urgency cannot be overstated, count as an invitation to take the political seriously in its conversation with faith? And conversely, would that dialogue have no consequence for the very intelligibility of Revelation?

Globalization disrupts the whole planet, spreads perplexities everywhere, and similar fears are rife between North and South. Even though it is advisable to understand and to confront them in their context, even though their foreseeable outcomes differ, similar questions are raised on both sides of the demarcation line – which some, furthermore, would see turned into an airtight wall! The question, to take only one, of intermediate bodies – that is of subsidiarity, and of the capacity for every person to be an agent in their history and in the development of all – applies equally in both hemispheres. Are we or are we not to take the gamble of structuring them and of reinforcing their structuring? Are we or are we not, in the public debate, to give their rightful place, in keeping with their real weight, to families, groups and associations, not just as a cluster of bodies but as a conjugation of freedoms and hopes? Are we or are we not going to understand that they offer the antidote to the ascendancy of monolithic value systems?

During the final decades of the twentieth century, several countries of the South underwent an extremely traumatizing period during which respect for the individual, for the poor, for social groups and for the land was grossly undermined. It provoked a strong political awareness and an outstanding social creativity. How can the energy that emerged in those days of struggle and oppression be sustained today, in the face of new issues such as tackling accelerated development and anarchic improvement in standards of living for some, and for others of controlling growth stagnation and the rise of corruption? What means, to what end, and in what time frame?'

The questioning is undeniably transversal. It is no less urgent in the North. How is one to promote a political direction under the shadow of a fallacious economic realism, a supposed managerial pragmatism, dismissing ideas and long-term views on the basis of 'It is all one'? Once public life is reduced to opinion surveys, the fabrication of bogus narratives, electoral campaigns and oratorical sparring that descend into smearing or deriding the opponent? When lawmaking amounts to the protection of vested interests, and the dealing of justice to an exercise that is erratic at best, and loaded at worst? When each citizen comes to the conclusion that the chief battles to be fought are personal ones? There again, what means, to what end, and in what time frame?

Short of a sea change guided by the principles of self-restraint and of the common good, it is hard to imagine how, in the short term, human societies, whether rich or poor, democratic or oppressed, will enjoy genuine political debates that lead to genuine political proposals. Confronted with globalization, the same questioning grates on them: how to give meaning to a free and just solidarity that can bring people together? The answers may vary, but to deny the questioning is to reject the political.

People will recall the lively debates on this issue in the 1970s. The strong polarizations that followed no longer prevail, but the concerns raised then are not all obsolete. Work, social justice, the promotion of personal dignity, authority, equality between men and women, clericalism within the Church, the involvement of the laity in the shaping of the Church structures and in its mission – all count as so many Gordian knots that cannot be simply forgotten as though they have been resolved. I do not regret the ideological excesses of the past – far from it. But how to take account of what existed, identify what has moved on, draw the lessons of what has been undergone? Thinking and professing polarized views does not necessarily rule out building together.

Travel tends to heighten still further my concern for communion among the disciples of Jesus Christ. There is little true dialogue between Christians – remarkably, in view of the flowering of new Churches, often local, autonomous and evangelical. How to relate to them, and how to give thought to this relationship? Why do Catholics leave their Church to join them? What did they not find here? What are they seeking there? Is there some lesson to draw or to learn? And lastly, what image might the search for unity present, among so great a number of disparate communities?

With a view to adjusting its presence in the world, Christianity has to ask itself questions about its reorganization. On the one hand it has to revise its model of progress towards unity. But on the other it has to find ways of thinking in new terms about the linkage between proclaiming the Word and the state of society. The recent synods of bishops have opened up fundamental approaches for the future of evangelization by recalling the importance both of collegiality and of subsidiarity in the life of the Church.

The Order has its part to play here, and indeed an example to set in so far as it keeps a creative faith with its beginnings. Echoing God's own trust, we are called to put credence in people, in their potential for reason, for putting to work their power of communion, for standing up to what offends their dignity. This calls for a political commitment in the shape of a dual duty: to listen to the diversity of the range of hope that dwells in the world, and to offer our own for the world's attention. A preacher cannot fight shy of taking such a plunge into the seething heart of humanity. There sound the first tentative phrases of the great tale of hope to which he wishes to bear witness.

Growing familiar

But where to begin? The family is in itself a Gospel, Good News within the Church and in the world. In its every aspect, it bears the human community at the heart of humanity in communion. It is the locus of the language in which the little human finds her- or himself unconditionally welcomed, to acquire the word meant for its hearing, and to live by it. There they learn the grammar of the basic relationships: to be daughter or son, brother or sister, mother or father. There they acquire the vocabulary of friendship and sociability. There they undergo their first joys and their first sorrows, births and bereavements, delights and heartbreaks, joinings and solitudes. The family is the place where one becomes human, becomes a believer. Rather than an end result of pastoral care, it is the original agent of evangelization. Hence it is the place where the Church first establishes itself.

As sacrament of salvation, the Church celebrates every phase of life that marks a milestone in family existence: initiation, reconciliation, marriage, funerals, thus instituting birth, forgiveness, marriage and death in the eyes of passing time transfigured by the grace of God. Those men and women spared by fate or by history know it for a miracle, and it is good that it should be so. But in the life of families there are also gay people, feuds, separated couples, abused women, neglected children, families exposed to hardship or exile, transgressive loves. How does the Church communion sit with them? What does it do to include them? How does it suffer from what happens to them? How does it draw strength from standing by them all in solidarity? The Church is not content merely to look on at what happens to them, it *is* in truth what happens to them. The joys and sorrows of families are joys and sorrows of the entire Church.

According to the philosopher Gabriel Marcel, 'to tell somebody "I love you" is to tell them "You will not die."' How does it happen that two people who used to love each other no longer do, sometimes to the point of hatred? How is it that a family that seemed bound for happiness sees itself destroyed? How do parents come to curse their children, and children their parents? How did the forever indissoluble find itself dissolved in an instant to the point of seeming dead, leaving in the pain of grief a promise of eternity?

What befalls each one of these befalls us all. It is in the light of communion that these dramas begin to emerge from the depths of their night.

The Church ought not so much to speak about as to give voice to those families who are the Church. The Church is family. It does not decide whether or not it wants to converse, but in serving the Word, it must converse within itself and with the world outside concerning what constitutes it, so rooted in this conversation is the passing-on of the faith. Relearning this will regain for evangelization a strength that it may have neglected for too long. Accordingly, in the days of the Synod on the Family called by Pope Francis, the Church has wanted to advance along the path where it grows closer to being the family of God.

Synodality is essentially an occasion of the Holy Spirit. Biblical, patristic and theological references, pastoral conceptions, political and moral philosophies, sociologies of secularization and enculturation: contrasted opinions have sometimes diverged to the point of seeming contradictory. The diversity of approaches and misgivings has made itself felt on several topics, among them views as to the situations of divorced and remarried couples, or how to come to terms with the reality of homosexual relationships. Cultural values certainly do not possess the power to transform nature, any more than moral values possess that of tailoring the person to their universal measure. But there are different forms of the politically correct. It is possible to dismiss as null and void the current debates concerning bioethics, genders, parenting, family and filiation. Likewise, one may seize upon these anthropological and societal shifts as so many chances to evangelize. Now here again, expertises aside, families will take precedence because their life is on the line. And beyond the hazards, confusions and splits that may mark their lived experience, always the same promise makes itself heard. Faithful is the God of the Covenant.

The now widespread brittleness of fidelity within marriage is an example. It can provoke judgements that would condemn it without appeal as a culpable weakness. But at the same time, because we are moulded in God's word, and we are grounded by the conversation that God conducts with us, we have to bear witness to Him who advises faithfulness even to the unfaithful. Our human commitments and our promises are entrenched in this Word of a God who wanted us able to be marks of His own commitment to fidelity, sealed by His Son. The Church wishes to give to future couples the joy of being called in this way to celebrate their love in the sacrament of marriage, but that delight is then not to be distinguished from the joy of evangelization. Contrary to an austerity verging on a withered legalism that all the more readily courts mischief, it is the whole life of each family that can etch its own history into God's long record with His people, with its joys and sorrows, its fidelities and splits, its achievements and its failures. This mystery is the very emblem of the presence of a 'loving God, faithful to humanity'. Within the spectrum of this mystery, how is one both to discern each individual pathway and to voice a theology of the Covenant promised to and with all?

Beyond the temptations to reduce it to false polarizations, the Synod did indeed achieve an approach accepting of uncertainties, hesitations and discords in its search for communion. The shared concern emerged that communion should remain essential so that the Church might further consolidate its unity by spreading the Gospel of the family. The learning of God, the tradition of the Church and the teaching of the Magisterium will be vital. But the most urgent challenge is for families to know themselves and actually to be the agents of the renewal for which Pope Francis is calling, in keeping with the whole Church tradition: to accompany humanity wherever it is by opening the pathways of mercy. God's companionship with humanity proves its truth in so far as it remains, in human history, forever incomplete. Incomplete because each family is called upon to offer its own share to the preaching. Incomplete because the Church, in step with all, is constantly required to set the table of mercy. Incomplete to the end of times, as the Dominican family also knows itself to be, which wishes as of now to proclaim the coming of the Kingdom.

Openness to difference

Wherever I go, once I am out of Europe, I am literally swamped by the vitality of the faith. Starting with Latin America, where the Dominican presence harks back to the Age of Discovery. It exerted on our brothers who first landed there a kind of instant fascination. They understood that Western culture, which might have been tempted to think itself alone in the world, was simply no such thing. That other cultures existed, rich in meaning, challenging and refined, foreign though they might seem. The preaching that accompanied that movement of expansion finally led, in the Order, to the theological rejection of slavery. This awakening enabled the spectacular evangelization of the peoples of that vast continent. It emerged no less covered with scars for having been subjected to military conflicts and civil wars, to dictatorships and brigandage, to nepotism and corruptions of every kind.

Latin America is enjoying a strong growth and great creativity liable to expose it to the front line of globalization, at a time when it continues to be prey to a reign of violence endemic in some places. But it remains buoyed up by the tremendous power of hope, bearing witness that the future holds a promise of life for all. It was, I believe, the strength of the Liberation theologies to have shown that humankind cannot be robbed of its future, because that future has a face, which is Christ's own.

In Ecuador, the Dominican Republic, Peru, Cuba, Colombia, Mexico and Argentina, the friars often established universities as soon as they arrived, thereby expressing their wish to contribute to the self-governing development of the indigenous populations. No doubt so as to pass on the faith, but above all to introduce the young people of these countries to the sharing of minds and to the challenge of education, that they might learn to give to others what they themselves were to receive. For their part, the brothers found a popular devoutness that was a lesson to their own piety and that continues boundless to this day.

Such a devoutness underlines both the need and the capacity among humans to make bonds with Him who created them, their desire to live in familiarity with a God who reveals Himself by making himself familiar. It is in this respect that such a devoutness can and must evangelize evangelization. It is not bidden to say what should be thought, or what should be done or said. It expresses the joy of the kerygma:[9] 'He exists, He came, He lived.' But in return, evangelization itself evangelizes devoutness so that it does not tailor God to the simple measure of our own outpourings.

This exchange between devoutness and evangelization goes on in Latin America, but it holds true, in reality, wherever the human seeks God. Such an exchange involves a people assembled, a daily relationship with God, a mystical reading of the life of Christ in the course of each existence, and the daring to welcome, to follow, and to love Him. The witness of the Latin-American churches invites the other churches in the world into such a rejoicing. The Church is always the beneficiary of a first evangelization.

At almost the same time as the New World, ancient Asia was one of the first mission destinations outside Europe for the Order, who also ventured early into the Pacific. From secularized Australia to the very Catholic Philippines, from divided Korea to Islamized Pakistan or to resolutely insular Japan, from barely accessible China to Timor, where we are freshly established, from India and Vietnam, where our

---

[9] 'The preaching of the Gospels; the element of proclamation as contrasted with didache (teaching) in the communication of the Christian gospel' (*New Shorter Oxford English Dictionary*) – Trans.

presence is solid, to Laos, Thailand and Sri Lanka, where mission is just starting, we number around a thousand brothers, one-third of them in training, some of these in Myanmar, formerly Burma, where we now have a base.

However, as in Latin America, and in Africa of course, I see in Asia – whether despite its unbridled economic growth or precisely because of it – globalization's transversal tragedy in action. Where are the people who do not matter? Not just where are they, what can we understand and say about them, and how might we help them, but first and foremost, in what way are we with them? You have only to pay a visit in the morning to the heaving outskirts of a megalopolis to know that there exist whole populations who count, alas, for next to nothing. They go unseen and unheard, and nobody seems to know how to make them seen and heard.

Perhaps it is owing to such a feeling of fatality that, on this continent of contrasts, the otherness of often hostile cultures plays out so forcefully, each with an intense quest for wisdom at its heart. The Order's priority is to establish a conversation between Christian theology and this whole profusion of philosophic, spiritual or mystical currents that adopt other manners of thinking. How is the Gospel message going to help this conversation to move towards communion? How can this desire to pass on the Gospel further a true and friendly dialogue? How is enculturation to be brought about between us? And how will all this incur the greatest possible respect for the rights of humanity?

This is the issue at stake for preaching in that region, which happens to overlap with globalization to the point of being scarred by it. We must take heed both of the gains achieved by intercultural or inter-religious dialogue, and of the risk of confinement run by closed identities that need to excel themselves. Our good fortune is that the missionary brothers and sisters have passed on this incentive to native brothers and sisters who thereafter enhance the understanding of these challenges on the basis of their own experience. What sort of specific face will the young Dominican brothers and sisters stemming from those cultures provide to the Order? How will they integrate the insights of their elders into the Order's own spirit of fraternity, in a conversation where each voice carries the same weight? How will they metabolize the tradition of the Order and pass it on to the world, beginning with themselves? How will they prompt the Order as a whole into solidarity in facing up to the challenges to peace and justice in these countries? I look forward to finding out. This venture affords a vital token for the future of the Preachers, but also for humanity's.

Gratitude for grace

Africa is no less decisive a continent for the future of the planet, and for the Dominicans it was likewise one of their first great zones of departure from their European cradle. The friars took the Gospel there, but the prodigious worlds and creatures that they came across repaid them a hundred times over for this contribution by guiding them in turn towards a more universal understanding of the faith. African cultures and the tradition of the Order are tightly knit together today. There were to be a thousand and one pages of exploits to record, brimming with light, celebration and gladness. But the peoples of the African continent remain, for many of them, in torment, and rather than to retail generalities, I prefer to relate here the kind of Holy Week that I went through in Bangui in the run-up to Easter 2015. More than ever at the time of that visit, it was not the Master of the Order who taught, but he himself who was taught. It happened like this.

From the moment of touchdown it was all desolation and bewilderment. The Central African Republic was barely emerging from the ethnic clashes that had ravaged it. Before my eyes spread a country struggling with that most terrible of scourges: the woeful memory of the evil that humans can inflict on other humans. The victim of political unrest, and hence rendered all the more fragile, the country was and would remain prey to the worst of violence. Like any living body that has been too roughly treated, it was running out of resources. Successive attempts by militias to seize power, followed by counter-attempts. Because of this vulnerability, all kinds of vote-rigging, domestic and external political pressure, the most sordid jockeying for power; could set off murderous explosions.

As Holy Week progressed, I experienced, in a flash of perception, the Mystery of the Passion. A flood of riotous convulsions locked into the gearing of death: the passion for power that began to tear everything apart, the passion for revenge that longed to destroy those who supposedly held power, the passion to manipulate religious identities to camouflage those cravings for power. It was all this that underwrote the claim, in a land where casual cohabitation between Christians and Muslim was commonplace, that here was a case of open conflict between the Quran and the Gospel. But they then staged the ethnic routine, on the basis of conspiracy theory: with such and such an identity supposedly threatening another such, it behoved the one to eliminate the other, and so on and on in a crazy tangle of final solutions. After months of accumulating conflicts, the country was bled dry – not a figure of speech.

Of some districts of Bangui there was nothing left: everything razed to the ground, with not one stone left standing on another. Mutual slaughter raged, through the crudest of means. They also procured guns, drugs, alcohol supplied by arms dealers into the grip of powerful forces that manipulated such clashes so as to entrench their own financial or ideological interests. In that beautiful country, as in so many others in Africa and elsewhere over the past decades, it was possible to see how morbid passions could break loose to destroy the individual whose existence seemed suddenly worthless.

Through our brothers we were receiving information about the griefs and losses afflicting every family, regardless of faith or culture. But knowing is one thing, seeing is another. Once in situ, how was anybody not to feel devastated in their turn by the denial of life that this unbridled violence led to? At the same time, though, and equally irresistibly, I could not fail to perceive the courage and resistance of the common people. I was particularly struck by the women, who found themselves in the front line. With all the men in jeopardy of lynching, it was they who must bury the dead, console the victims, care for the wounded, hide the adolescents and protect the children. Equally it was their voices that broke the deadly hush fallen on Bangui. I found myself listening to utterly overwhelming stories of faith and life.

Among a thousand sacrifices by some people to save others is the remarkable story of this woman who never lost hope in the miraculous. Her Muslim neighbours had to flee after the destruction of their house. Her Christian neighbours were attacked by another gang of looters. At first she wanted to stay on so as to keep on tending her livestock and be able to continue feeding her family. Then she realized that, all around her, a person's life counted for less than the flesh of a domestic animal. So she and her nearest and dearest left, the adults forming a protective cordon to prevent militias from kidnapping their young people. They walked on, using their mobiles to avoid ambushes in which they would have been captured or killed. Along the way, this woman never stopped telling God: 'You must protect us.' And He did, she confided, stilling the terror of the gloomy tale on her lips with the light in eyes that shone with faith.

That faith, I heard and saw it, dazzling, there before me in a Bangui shattered by inconceivable griefs. The reality of an Easter-tide land in the throes of a radical, absurd and inhuman hostility. The reality too of the victory of the human spirit and of faith over violence. This woman was able to tell me that she put her life at risk in order to save life in the making by pursuing her conversation with God. And her God saved her. If all this could happen – the trust of a woman, her care for her kin, the solidarity of friendship, the presence of God – we can believe that the world is not the prey of evil but that it has truly been saved.

Against the temptation of revenge stand all those who want to break the hellish circle of violence. They are far many more than is recognized. Laypeople, unbelievers and believers, follow the priests who repeat in the words of an Archbishop: 'Whoever want to avenge themselves must be protected from themselves.' They mediate between their own folk and their yesterday's adversaries, these last under threat after being the threat, and saying: 'No, you will not kill him. Kill him, and you kill me too.' There is no calculated heroism here, but a reflex of faith and of humanity that declares: 'I protect your humanity as it is also mine.'

That Holy Week in Africa further impressed on my mind the conviction that salvation lies in the fact that our God comes among us to take our humanity upon Himself, and to resist – at the very core of humanity – our capacity for inhumanity. The God who made Himself vulnerable to the denial of God faced our emptiness to the point of dying of it and rising again from within it. That power of Salvation goes to the heart of what has to be re-created. We say that the passion of Christ and

His Resurrection save us from sin and from death, but the proper purpose of Salvation, for God, is to save the human from the inhuman.

In Bangui I realized, to my shame, that too often I have forgotten the endless reach of the Creator's crazy love for His creature. God, in the person of the Son, came to humanity in that uttermost plight when, suddenly overtaken by itself, it finds itself swamped by the passion to destroy itself. It was in this that He was wounded, through this that He was killed. But as I was told one day in Haiti by a young Christian who was also at odds with the senseless violence of a dictatorship of lies: you cannot kill the Resurrection.

And neither can we be made to betray charity. Through the mystery of Christ's Passion, we are together in humanity, in frailty as well as in salvation. It is not only that the Order and Africa are one. The fact is that the Order owes Africa a debt.

Not to go in fear

The duty that the Master of the Order bears of visiting every province, to bring the fraternal gaze that Dominic desired, has given me a fresh eye for the lands of my birth, which I had believed I knew well. It was not so. To whoever casts a fresh eye over it, Europe is larger and more diverse than Europe alone. Here the Preachers meet the major challenge of having the Gospel rediscovered by a world that was shaped by it, has in part ignored it, and yet goes on believing that it knows it. The task today is to reinvent ways to announce the same Good News, so that the Old Continent may learn anew that what it deems its past determines its future.

The twentieth century, with its succession of heinous wars and murderous ideologies, marked a new stage in European history. But the hope of building peace together after horror is mingling now with a ubiquitous economic liberalism, the illusion of an overriding hedonism, the temptation of identitarian separation and ambivalence towards the influx of migrants. The cynics envisage a minimal union that anyone could get on board with, while cultivating diverse reservations and disconnects of an economic, cultural or religious kind by dint of permanent horse-trading over divergent interests. Yet Europe has very good reasons to want to be Europe. Its problem is that the secularization – defamiliarization with the great religious narratives – that dominates her blots out, by means of facts on the ground, the diversity that it promotes in theory.

The European continent is a fascinating place for its cultural memories, but also for the convictions of lore and cult whose source they are. Essential to its construction, they are proving to be indispensable to its reconstruction. We know very well that the old Europe was the theatre of ceaseless wars, of terrible divisions and destruction, exclusions, manipulations and repeated land grabs – for religious reasons among others, or at least instrumentalizing religion. But it is also the land where, in the wake of those tragedies, peoples who would have had every reason to hate each other decided to repent and to become allies. It is this movement of critical return to itself that made it possible to perceive a future for all, in the conviction that the spirit of conflict should not prevail and have the final word. To put it another way, the Europeans proved able to oppose to the fatality of violence a form of hope, which is never to be found without some mystique of unity.

That is why, at the very heart of the journey that Europe is undertaking today, the religious convictions that moulded it and that remain hardy there still cannot be dismissed. They have their word to say, in that they too constitute representations of the world, of society, of the future to be desired. Their expression is vital precisely inasmuch as no one intends to give up a secular lifestyle that can guarantee genuine freedom of conscience, valid for each and everybody. In several countries of the Old Continent, and in spite of sharing the same citizenship, people seem too willing to foreclose their conversation on the pretext of divergences about innermost convictions so basic as to render them utter strangers to one another. Unblocking the jams that preclude reciprocal knowing, esteem and respect is all the more necessary because without such endeavours, the culture of solidarity by which Europe might teach lessons to the rest of the world will remain a pious wish.

The Old Continent itself is not monolithic, and in both its central and its eastern regions faith retains a powerful popular voice, renewed by the memory of Soviet communism's still recent persecutions. Further west the future of the religious orders causes concern in view of the rather scanty number of vocations. All the more so by comparison with postwar figures whose exceptional scale we no doubt underestimate. All the same, to fixate on statistics is to overlook the essential. Modest in size, the Order of Preachers has a regular intake of enough new friars, albeit unevenly distributed over countries, to assure its true vocation, which is creativity in the field of evangelization. The first aim of the Preachers is not to plough ahead come what may, but rather not to shirk their proper charism. Following in Dominic's footsteps, the Order lives so as to be the servant of God's dialogue with His people. At this moment in the history of that 'Old Europe', perhaps even more than on other shores, the Church cannot shy away from the call to explore new ways of life for Christians – ways that pay proper attention to the hope inside them.

Referring to the demography of a religious body in the midst of a secularized universe also calls for making a lucid approach to the demands of ageing, and of what comes with it. Growing old is neither an illness nor a sin, but nor is it necessarily a merit. It is merely a fact of life. How to give each elderly brother his rightful place, while also making room for each new brother? This is a high-wire exercise because it puts youthful creativity and the capacity of age to pass on what it knows to the test of solidarity between the generations. How the Church and the Order deal with this matter is bound to exert its effect on European societies where this question will grow ever more acute in the decades to come. They themselves will be judged on the harmonious cohabitation that they have or have not abetted between their young and their elders.

This transformation in the age pyramid is critical, but there is no cause to fear it. The maturity of experience does not in itself confer the privilege of wisdom or of contemplation, nor the keenness of fresh eyes that of being automatically correct about the need for action. More broadly, the major issue in apostolic creativity, in Europe as everywhere else, lies in the tension between continuity and innovation. The Order's history is already long, its institutions many and established. The dialectic it has managed to foster during its eight centuries of life between landmarks elapsed and prospects still to come resides in the image of the coming of the Kingdom, which is fulfilled here and now in the uniqueness of the Eucharist.

Conversion by conversing

The picture would not be complete without the brothers and sisters of Northern America. Whereas the Canadian province must still endure the waiting time of a tree in winter, the provinces of the United States are displaying a healthy dynamism. All are at the heart of a Church distinguished by a broad array of cultures, which offer an exacting challenge to evangelization. Thus the Order is present in the midst of that culture world that exerts an unprecedented global influence and spreads a liberal but often materialist conception of humanity. This raises a challenge and a worry that extend far beyond the Atlantic basin, something that North American Christendom is well aware of, inured as it is – and here lies one of its great strengths – to debating it openly.

There also exist, in this far North, a poverty and hardship that marginalize the little people even more, seeing that abundance seems to reign there. Globalization leaves its imprint everywhere. It does not operate only between rich and poor, between developed and emergent countries, but also within each one of them. There is not a single nation that does not count more and more numerous social groups who feel to some degree humiliated and forgotten. The rift is also internal, and first of all cultural, opposing the arrogance of the affluent to the dereliction of the nowhere people, granting that there might be a natural tolerance for inequality and endorsing the partition of the world between top side and underside.

It is the chief responsibility of those countries that once led worldwide scrambles for expansion, or that now parade the attributes of power, to remedy this sense of resignation. The price of their dominance was paid by the others. It consisted in the contempt or neglect shown to those under occupation, and sometimes also, alas, in their extortion. The West must not lose the memory of its excesses, when it has learned in the meantime the price of watching evil grow banal. In the name of this exacting remembrance, past all consolation, it seems to me that the duty of Christendom in this hemisphere, more than anywhere else, is to forestall the raging drive towards blind conquests.

Furthermore, the preaching of the Gospel in the 'West' that makes up North America and Europe for the rest of the world has special difficulties to contend with. The movements of migration that feed it, originally unleashed and instrumentalized in aid of production, are growing exponentially, and demand from the Church a redoubled pastoral care, cultural adaptation and social flexibility. At the same time, the Church retains the mission to reach out to local populations who have learned to grow indifferent to the life of faith, and to forget that all-embracing community is essential to Christianity. It must also enter into dialogue with the techno-scientific world whose advances keep on transforming the relation of humankind both with the world and with itself.

It is on this final point that the proclaiming of the Kingdom requires the utmost creativity, so clearly do the changes bring unforeseeable consequences. Faced by the cumulative mastery over living matter, from birth to death, what wisdom will prevail, that enables humans to fulfil their humanity in an ambience of critical and humble friendship concerning their powers? To researchers who aspire to establishing a new transhumanity, by augmenting unbridled the potentialities of the human to the point of arousing the dream of immortality, what conversation does the Good News have to open? In respect of the social networks and of their new empire in which everyone must tweet, how to promote a freedom that is not solitary practice, a communion that is neither identitarian nor anonymous, an existential span that resists the ephemeral?

Nor are there simple answers to more immediate topics. World economics imposes the damaging power of finance upon the earth's ecology. A just theology will see to it that economic criteria alone do not determine apostolic and pastoral choices. The global destruction of identities is triggering a backlash of reconstructed identitarian movements. A healthy ecclesiology will prevent squaring communitarianism with credibility, given that the Christian's security hangs not on the return to an idealized past, but on hope in the future and, even more, on the assurance of eschatology.

That the Friar Preachers belong to one and the same Order, whereas they hail from different and sometimes conflictual realms, compels them to proclaim the Gospel as a common good. The proclamation of the Kingdom consists – witness the very words already spoken by Paul – in the unheard-of contention that henceforth there can be 'neither Jew nor Greek' (Rom. 10: 12; 1 Cor. 12: 13; Gal. 3: 28; Col. 3: 11). This message is not for another age, for days gone by. To be sure, disparities exist within the Dominican family, as they do in the world at large. But they constitute good news within the Good News, since they signal to the Preacher the call to commit to a deep approach of communion, and thus of conversion, which makes up his life, bearing this memory as something yet to come.

To bridle terror

The rise in violence is worldwide. Likewise it takes many forms. Its expressions do not all fall under the rather vague heading of 'religious revival', any more than fundamentalisms all amount to Islamism. Nevertheless, in one decade the jihadist terror has spread from the East to every continent, sowing death and fear wherever it goes. The very mechanism of this phenomenon is, as the name suggests, to provoke fear, to stoke distrust, to arm an identity-based defence reaction that will ensure its spread and increase. Faced with this vicious circle, one of the key considerations is to know whether we, on both sides, will be able to sustain a conversation. I think and hope so. But that ambition will be all the more genuine for having set out to define the relevant questions.

Is it possible to essentialize a religion and to reduce its many centuries of history to its present-day upheavals? Can a whole mass of believers be incriminated for the unacceptable breaches of human dignity carried out in its name by refractory minorities? Can one overlook the disconnect between the faith professed with regard to humankind, and the ethos observed between peace and warlike gestures of destruction and passion? For a Christian, whoever claims to exercise power in the place of God is departing from the truth. Jesus died for having displayed that fact once and for all. It is this gaze that a Christian has to cast on a Muslim today, and so see to it that they are not ostracized, banished from humanity and dehumanized in their turn, which is precisely the objective.

Many are the barriers that stand in the way of this view. Islam is bidden to anathematize Islamism. Many Muslim authorities have condemned it unreservedly, and I cannot see in what name they might be required to do so more than they already have. Islam is urged to declare whether its God accepts killing. Many an off-the-cuff commentator embarks upon second-hand theologies combining a few Quranic verses and the odd canonical reference without ever going into the life experience of the faithful, and I am at a loss to see how they themselves could be held immune to a form of fanaticism. Qualified speakers are called for, but only to instantly stress the lack of them. And yet is it so certain that somebody who wished to discuss their doctrine with Catholics, the Orthodox or Protestants would easily find spokespersons up to the task of discussing their doctrine? And would it not grow clear that the views of experts do not preclude the existence of factions and fallings-out over opinions? Christianity itself is far from unequivocal, not only in its statements about the faith but also in its political positions, its views about money, its respect for the freedom of the person, its desire to progress towards unity, in its relationship with other religions, and its approach towards the future of the world.

What do such questions mean? Deep down, this involves an abstract idealization of the religious fact. It is expected to convey the hold that God exerts over human live, whereas what it actually displays is the wish people have to convey God. It forgets the words of the Son of God that enjoin the hearer not to 'tie up heavy burdens and lay them on people's shoulders without lifting a finger to move them' (Matt. 23: 4). At the same time, whether or not there exists a leader, a hierarchy, a clergy, are we not precisely at that hour the world over, when every believer is deemed responsible for their faith? Accordingly, the right question is rather to know whether we belong to the same human communion, whether it is up to us to cultivate our common humanity, and whether we all do not feel the selfsame thirst for a human solidarity.

With each attack that drenches the earth with blood, I am minded of the saying of Saint Paul that 'inside the body each part may be equally concerned for all the others. If one part is hurt, all the parts share its pain'(1 Cor. 12: 25–6). After every act of terror, I note the outbursts of general indignation, and that they find simple ways of affirming that what happens to one of us happens to all of us. Here is the only force that can stand up to terror; it is the whole of humanity that is wounded, that rebels against it, and says no in the name of a single, shared and mutual dignity; and only this spirit of reciprocity can help us to listen to reason, and give us the strength not to allow ourselves to be locked into universal hostility. The world belongs to all, and we are its keepers together.

That does not make it a matter of pitting a naive otherworldliness against a simplistic demonization. The state of terror caused by jihadism likewise raises two political urgencies that need to be addressed without delay. The first involves international relations and chancelleries. The democracies of the northern hemisphere cannot give in to the single logic of war into which terror strives to goad the world. Neither can they maintain the false strategic compromises that for too long have been seeking to protect purely material interests, the cynical mercenary collusion in these conflicts under the guise of wanting to avoid them. The proof exists of the tragic outcome of such calculations.

The second urgency is internal. The same democratic states are dragging their feet over providing a culture of social cohesion that would, in the long term, pay heed to the new diversity in their populations. The fact must be acknowledged that some sizeable population groups feel, rightly or wrongly, a kind of constant existential humiliation that in turn causes a clamorous quest for identity. The sense of being marginal can then give rise to the will to self-marginalize.

Vulnerability to manipulation also plays a part in this rejection of the law. Walls of estrangement are going up in the peripheral housing estates because these very peripheries are being abandoned by the centres. The impossibility of recognition brings about the non-recognition that encourages hostility. Breaking with this logic does not come about through speeches or debates, but through a true political determination to promote education and solidarity, together with acts of comfort and compassion.

Seeking new bearings

It is the same logic of separation that prevails in the Middle East. This cradle of the earliest writing would be handicapped forever if its Christian lung were to disappear. It would find itself historically and culturally amputated. That is the risk in Iraq or in Syria, in a climate of warfare, but also in the Levant, where the threat of persecution is spreading, and with it the temptation to remove themselves, for those to whom the West owes the passing-on of the Gospel and of the faith.

We know this, but what do we do? Who will dare to tell a father that he must expose his wife and children to slaughter on the basis of a museum conception of the past? After he and his family have fled death, survived as refugees in concrete bunkers, under makeshift tents, with neither baggage nor protection – how could anyone explain to them that it is their duty to go home to a country where there is no law but the gun? As for ourselves, will we succeed in understanding that we would seal their fate by isolating them from the whole region's other populations, whether majorities or minorities? The Christians of the West cannot weep for the Christians of the East only in the light of the fate that Muslims have in store for them. The Western powers cannot ask Eastern Christians to stay put unless they pledge support for their safety.

Now, the loss of the very notion of neighbourliness explains the current crisis. Some Muslims, some Christians, once riverside neighbours and even – and more often than imagined – friends, find themselves swallowed up in antagonistic loyalties. Manipulated by supposedly religious forces, they have ceased to believe that it is possible for them to live together, or at least side by side. Am I more pleasing to the Prophet if I go to loot the house opposite with a cross on its lintel? Plainly, that is not true. And all know this, including those who claim not to. Thus a new tolerance of evil has come about, in the acceptance of murderous divisions.

Our brothers in the Levant speak with sorrow about the loss of ancestral linkages that were not always idyllic but that did not allow for the feeling of such an irretrievable divorce. In doing so they also recall the memory of a time not in key with fatality. Their speech is like a flare in the night. It has never been easy for people to live in communion, and all the less so in this Middle East of such a complex history and geography. But to my knowledge it is not they, the Orientals, and in no case they alone, who enacted the demarcation of borders, the partition of peoples and tribes, and the form of the regimes and alliances that determine the dreadful and perilous present. The Western powers contributed to it – certainly not the Eastern powers without them, but neither was it of Eastern prompting, with their consent and on their behalf. Always at some point or other comes the reminder of humanity's common responsibility for humanity's affairs.

Too often, Middle Eastern tensions are narrated with the blame laid on a single opponent, which is cast as irreconcilable. 'They' are the culprits, the intransigents, the enemies of humankind. Everybody has their own offender. But such a mechanical and Manichean designation of the enemy ought no longer to exist. We should know that history is common to all of us. To presume that there is a them and an us, irretrievably, is to refuse to see that there is a human community of error here, that we are all both offenders and victims, that the past extends into the present, and that in wishing to banish humankind from humankind we amplify its damaging effects. So, as in the days of Hispaniola, there is no choice but to accept that among so many places gone astray, so is the West.

Now in the meantime, what of our brothers and sisters who live in the Middle East, who bear witness there to preaching, and who reject the inevitability of division? They act in peace. Regardless of who is who, they dare to pick up babies in their arms, embrace the elderly in mourning, find a roof, food and a blanket for men and women alike, and reopen the schools to welcome children. They care for human beings, whoever they are, because they are in pain. There are wounded memories that have to be repaired. There is the most primordial memory of friendship that has to be revived. This is their way of resisting.

And they are the best placed to know how arduous such a task is. They do not lock themselves into the aridity of an interfaith dialogue that would be purely intellectual. Such a dialogue, they know from experience, is never easy. Often it looks to them like a minefield, wide open to interference, exposed to the falsehoods of power, be they conscious or unconscious. These brothers and sisters give of themselves. They may not do better or more than others do, but their presence conveys what the Church is. In these situations where human life is so endangered, they put their own on the line as the only true possible response.

The first compassion lies in the consolation that can be offered. That consolation is also a consolidation.

There is no real hospitality or true charity without the active protection of the weakest against the temptations or the ills that they endure. That rule holds good on both sides of the Mediterranean – here inner-city youth, there displaced families. It also applies both in North and sub-Saharan Africa and in the Americas and Asia. In the Middle East we do want Christianity to remain, not simply for remaining's sake, but so that it should display there, in line with its vocation, a real, close-knit, fraternal presence of the transcendence that does not fear death. So that it should communicate the readiness to cross the line, the courage of friendship.

Our brothers and sisters are present in fact to take care of the human, to console the living, to look the other in the eye, and always to bow before Him whom the Semitic and Greek liturgies celebrate as the axis of the world, the Christ who is 'the Orient, the sun of justice, master of light unfading'.

Bear witness and pass on the faith

Good or bad? When referring to globalization, people seem happy to reel off its positive or its negative outcomes. The proper question should instead be to determine whether, and how, this general transformation in the state of the world, already in full spate, can work in the service of all. Which comes down to asking ourselves how this movement impacts on the least common denominator as an absolute criterion of the common good. How does it take account of those who do not count? The prerequisite here is that the nations invite to their round table those women and men that they still find too easy to forget.

Is this a utopian view? To hope is also to be patient and stubborn. By enabling us to draw inspiration from the Creator of everything to which He gives the breath of His Spirit, to hope is to trust in the creative capacity of humankind. To hope is to have the courage to confront and to understand failures, the better to take to the road again. To hope is never to forget the richness of the seed that falls to ground. Sometimes we survey how far we have strayed from the grace of hope, and sadness would come close to overwhelming us if this spur were not sharp enough to rekindle that breath of life which, in the proper sense, enthuses us.

Those who suffer are before, behind, beside us. They are with us and we with them. We and they, they and us, are interdependent. And yet we prefer to ignore that awkward existence, to deny that mutual dependence. Just as our culture flouts people so as to carve up the earth that feeds them, loots their resources, exploits their labour and cashes in on their strife. Rather than see this reign of sorrows extend worldwide, the great opportunity of globalization could on the contrary be as a school of compassion, but a compassion driven by the active awareness that it has to serve the human communion – and serve it fully. By embracing the spurned dignity of the misused, the degraded dignity of whoever forgets the good.

That there is an interdependence of dignities is one of our most common experiences. Who is there who has never felt themself humiliated by observing the humiliation endured by another? Who has never been shaken to the depths of their humanity by the sight of another's humanity defiled? Does the spectacle of rage not disturb us by inspiring a double backlash of feeling, both towards those who inflict it and those who endure it? So many of the world's tragedies arise from a desertion of the human that is spreading like an inferno.

So does evangelization, through which the Church grows to become what it is and truly wishes to be, find itself called to open a dialogue with globalization in order to give their place – first and foremost – to the last, which is to say the greatest number, at the beating heart of God's people. Not in a face-off but in the familiarity of a friendship that rules out no conversation. Especially with the young. Those who pass harsh judgements on the behaviours of the younger generations make a grave mistake. They are blamed for not committing in the long term, but nothing in the world today either lasts or is intended to last. On top of the general feeling of shallowness, young people have to face the further worry of not knowing what shape times to come are going to assume, what place they will be given in the future.

What the long term does hold is suffering, but these are also the hopes. We must listen to the young's concerns and give them our unconditional trust if we are to restore some credibility to the world. In order to be agents in the future, they have to be backed in their capacity to be agents in the present. Education remains beyond dispute a priority for whoever desires to respect and care for humanity. It is not aimed solely at the learners, but represents a gift made to human communities. It institutes the human in a position to pass on what it values. It is an act of tradition. To reinvent the aspects of life by supporting the new organization of the world through its educational systems – this seems to me the best way to resist dislocation.

This poses a prophetic challenge. Education, in the sense of the training of the critical capacity, is an urgent priority. A true educational project does not only entail the handing down of a body of knowledge that has grown to the point of putting the notion of a global general knowledge out of reach. It must also pass on the propensity, the courage and the joy to think for oneself, in an age that readily confuses consensus with uniformity, the opinion of the moment with thinking firmly rooted in critical rigour. At the other extreme, the illusion consists in telling everyone that they must think on their own, by and for themselves. It is a present-day reflex to isolate each person in the solitude of their own individuality, on the pretext of an absolute respect for the person. Only let war disappear, and all would be for the best in the best of all possible worlds, each and every one with their own opinions and with no more real social relations. This false idea of tolerance would lead at best to mutual indifference, at worst to the tacit acceptance of the unacceptable. It would ratify the power of a few over the greater number. It would create a society where sociability would look suspicious.

Both thinking to order and thinking in isolation are versions of non-thinking. They have as their respective counterparts relativism and fundamentalism. It is not possible to think in monologue, for thought puts the subject in relation to the other, and supposes exchanges. The path of education assumes that every person reaches the conclusion that they need to be taught to think, and that they had best get started straight away, and so throw off their isolation. It is because transmission is fragile that truth sets free. In this sense, any intellectual apprenticeship also entails an ethical initiation.

But there too, in the moral sphere, to witness and to pass on happen in a different way than we might suppose. There is what the transcendent God says of Good and Evil. There is what we sense of it by instinct, which surfaces compellingly from within and makes us surpass ourselves without having to name Him. Continually, we ascertain that one human is worth all humans, and that the greatest spiritual rigour tallies with the plainest facts of being human. This assertion is a call to resistance, for wishing to restore the conditions of universal dignity. And yet, this is not a question of picking a model of action out of a catalogue of organizations offering good works and justice, but rather of leaving oneself open to the love of Christ, and then contemplating it. Not indeed of bearing our crosses to signal our resignation to the suffering of the world, but of seeing at the heart of those sorrows Christ, hanging from the mystery of the Cross, and joining Him to live out this mystery beside Him.

We stand today at a turning point in the life of the Church when evangelization will renew itself to the extent that it opens conversations with the greatest numbers. We witness the example of Pope Francis, who makes a point of speaking personally to everyone, and who is personally engaged in his every word. What does he say? Simple things with simple words. Starting with the fact that it is possible, in oneself and with others, to believe and to live by the Gospel. He does not deliver a speech that is the institution addressing the world, he delivers the conviction of a believer in the midst of the world. He dares to express what stirs in all of us: the power of God's mercy, who in His care for His Creation strives to foster humanity, bringing it together in unity.

If Jesus truly chose to give His life so that the world should be in communion, then we in turn must put our own in play. In this way, all will feel the profound delight of being able to draw deep on the fire of their evangelical desire. I feel that I am saying nothing unusual here that the brothers do not say themselves. I have the conviction that such is the determination of the Preachers. Deep down, perhaps that is what it is, to wish to devote one's life to the given Word.

Hoping against hopelessness

What I see in the course of my travels and encounters is that humans will never be the same in the terms of the native land and mother tongue that preside over their birth or their life. But they will always be the same as the other humans living in what seem to them the confines of their own universe. The diversity is concrete, powerful and deep, but it does not signify that one can speak in terms of a juxtaposition of reciprocal indifferences – any more than of a supposed equality of risks and of suffering.

It is not that all cults and all cultures are being bamboozled, but that all of them are open to it. All the same, no cult, and no culture, risks the same manipulation. That goes too for the solidarities that civilizations can seal among themselves, but also for the cracks that may split them from within. It is this twin movement of explosion and implosion that we are observing today. The rule of violence that ensues seems to have the covert design of quelling compassion.

Now the most arresting feature of moving around the world comes from realizing just how much one human feels for the other. A jolt of humanity stirs in the emotion I feel at what another person feels, the desire that overtakes me to walk beside them through the trials they are facing, the sense of how imperative it is to prove our communion to them. In this very world of tribulations there lurks an underside of pain and sorrow. And it echoes with the call that is made to me to care for the other, inasmuch as I trust the other to hear the call to care for me. This exchange that goes without words, that makes do with little, and is content with a meeting of eyes, the bending of a back, the spread of a hand, makes us kindred.

This awareness warrants that division and confrontation cannot be the final words in the story of humanity. That it cannot be so. That one person could not sanctify the dehumanization of the other. That is why the betrayal of the human capacity for caring and trust is so grievous. To falsify it – were it only out of negligence – imperils all humanity. The work of the Divider is to have humankind believe that it is for ever fated to wage war with humankind. He, the 'murderer from the start' (John 8: 44), deploys every wile to this end. Perpetually he strives to regenerate evil, so that the propagation of hell should seem to prove him right, should crop up as the ultimate horizon. Such is the special gift of the Divider, to instil to the point of despair the impossibility of salvation. Each one of us can be caught in the web of his lies at any moment, and at any moment, too, every one of us must work against him by detecting his tricks and dispelling his illusions.

But how to succeed here by our human lights? The dual impulse of spiritual discernment and intellectual lucidity is essential, but it is not enough. It takes more – a different light, that comes from somewhere else. Entry into the Covenant that God proposes amounts to striking up the dialogue between the creature's faculty of compassion and the infinite mercy of Him who created her. And thus to experiencing the power of that mercy that springs from 'the bowels of our God' (Luke 1: 78; see also Isa. 63: 15),[10] moved to see

---

[10] Quoted from the Douay-Rheims translation. Most English translations are more euphemistic.

His people in slavery, which alone can yield anew, and for always, the human in all of its liberty.

Every Preacher aspires to attune to this dynamic of resistance to division, to reweave humanity from its underside, to do as Jesus did. He who achieves unity in abundance, and who truly brings peace, will be neither me nor another, but Him. Preaching is that: to dare to say that, as against all despair, one hopes in Him.

5

Unfolding the Mystery

Self-divesting

How else to act and to speak, than by returning again and always to the source of the Holy Preaching? Keeping the vision of Dominic intact and fruitful supposes that we live the mystery of the Church without obsessing about figures and productivity, structures and outcomes. Sometimes it seems to me that, in step with the modern trend, the Church has admitted the institution of a consumerist model that targets individual states of mind, whereas its task is to lead the way to free interchange in fraternal communities. But it is not a factory geared to the production and distribution of sacrament on demand and made to measure. In the wake of the revelation that unfolded at Emmaus, it is when the Church builds on encounters to celebrate God's presence that it makes itself a place of salvation.

The essence of the Church is not that it should succeed in its projects, it is that it takes on what humanity takes on. That it makes it its own, so that the grace of Christ may then do its own work. This asks us to shift the paradigm of evangelization and to make ruthless evaluations of the pastoral responsibilities we assume. More brothers than I thought are in charge of parishes where they often do fine work. But the logic of management should not take precedence over the imperative of the Christian community to witness, and the risk exists that no time or energy is left to devote to the sole essential. At Emmaus, the sharing of the bread comes at the end. The Eucharist is the most precious gift because the Church is communion, and it is as communion that it celebrates it.

The difficulty, when founding a movement, is to not institutionalize what has been founded. There is a strong tension between the charism of itinerancy proper to the preacher and the urge to settle down, quickly established in minds and in actions as a permanent given. The Desert Fathers privileged voluntary exile so as to assure themselves of the status of stranger. Which Benedict XVI called 'self-expropriation' as a spiritual path to the 'new evangelization'. Or which Pope Francis means when he advises to 'go to the peripheries' and to avoid 'self-referentiality'. The effort of detachment has always lain at the heart of the Order.

All that we have established over the centuries had the purpose of having the power of communion shine at its brightest. The Transfiguration is communicative in itself. It enlightens and it kindles. The sanctuaries, parishes, universities, schools and welfare or health centres that we have created or directed were not ends in themselves. They were, for us, places of support and education in the faith where all could learn to know themselves alive by putting trust in the Living One, by going to draw for themselves on the deepest of the Wellspring, by attaining the freedom that makes them over in God's divine likeness.

When the purpose of such structures falls to becoming their own perpetuation, they resemble the black holes in galaxies that swallow all matter around them for their own enlargement. Dead themselves, they grow deadly. Keeping them as they are for the love of the past or for fear of the future does harm to the service they were sworn to. And yet no structure is eternal. The only rightful perpetuity lies in the movement that arises from the ever-reborn openness of Communion. The very process of mission calls for brothers who came from far away to take their leave once the moment arrives for new brothers native to the area to take their turn to preach. And then one day they too will go elsewhere, and further . . .

This shift is inherently difficult, because it is never easy to abandon the settled position, to give up what exists, to strip away the security, false though it be, suggested by permanence. All of the works we have achieved, splendid as they may be, run the risk, we know, of turning one day into clutter that clouds our sight and hearing and blocks our way, preventing us from meeting the challenge of the hour, where Christ is waiting. Our new brothers, arriving from other worlds than that of historical Christendom, and who have forsaken riches under the spell of the Gospel, are here to help us to stiffen the will for movement. By contrast with the present day's restlessness, the craving for ever more possessions and sensations, the spiritual exodus supposes a withdrawal from the self to embrace the other. Which it is possible to do, if only one follows the path of the All-Other.

Taking the chance

Are not the world and history deprived of God's presence, precisely in the sense that the present day's humanity lives more and more as if this same God did not exist? This question is all-important for any whose wish is to proclaim the approach of the Kingdom. A long and rigorous labour of analysis remains to be undertaken in order to appraise both its meaning and its scope. The secularization attended by a certain

'defamiliarization from God' that is bestriding the
northern hemisphere is making equal progress in the
southern. It can be found both in Africa and in Asia.
It is not exclusive to North America but affects South
America too. It is not confined to Western Europe, but
extends into Central and Eastern Europe. Everywhere
the distinction widens between society and religion.
More and more, the new cultures are dispensing with
the ancient faiths, and people grow defamiliarized
from age-old allusions to transcendence or immanence,
and from the ancestral registers of the sacred and the
profane. I see in this disruption both an opportunity
and a risk.

The risk derives from suggesting that it is simply
a matter of a sickness to which believers hold the
remedy. The invariable temptation is to stigmatize
every change as a pathology. And it is also an anthropological constant to conjure up an adversary and then
to configure them as the polar opposite of one's own
self-image. The Church is not exempt from this when
it succumbs to declaring the sickness or to designating
the enemy, the better to justify the solutions it sees
fit. However, the transformation now under way
goes beyond the dialectical game between revolution
and reaction that has haunted the last two centuries.
Let us not be like the attendants of that gleaming
temple in Asia who, having displayed on its pediment
the slogan 'Jesus is the answer', found one morning the

message 'What is the question?' splashed on its façade. Secularization raises real issues and presents obvious dangers, but the chief risk remains that of responding to it without having taken the time and the effort to absorb the questions it raises.

What is the question? Here lies the opportunity, which is to hear out the needs and the dreams that our contemporaries express in asserting their autonomy. What thirsts and what hungers is the growing technical and scientific mastery of reality, of life and of the linkages among people, supposed to allay? What fears and what aspirations are displayed by the loss of credibility for institutions, of which mistrust of the Church is but one facet? How will attention paid to these critical trends lead us ever deeper into the heart of the Gospel of peace that we desire to proclaim? All this is an opportunity offered, in that it forces us to discard our fixed positions and comfort zones. It is the very aim of Evangelization.

What does this phenomenon say? That the human being has grown aware of their potential for intelligence and freedom, and intends to take charge of the organization of their world, their social life and underpinnings of existence in a relation that both critiques their heritage and nurtures their creativity. That they do not propose to invoke invisible and sovereign principles in order to do so. That they want to advance in autonomy without resorting to any kind of heteronomy. That this movement, which may include those women and men who do connect with God, collectively refrains from mentioning God. It is self-evident that such a transformation may shock. But viewed more closely, as it stands it should inspire nothing but admiration for the wisdom it reveals, and which is contained in Creation.

Its price is, patently, words, gestures and acts of refusal or denial of God, of disdain for God, and even of exclusion or persecution aimed at those who are bound to God. It happens that such affirmations arise in reaction to the excessive influence of the religious over the civil power, of the guidance of souls over the government of things, or of certain forms of spiritual presence attending the freedom of consciences, and they must then be deemed a useful reminder to draw distinctions among categories. But it also happens that, through ideology, it is proclaimed that God has no meaning. This poses the question of discourse and dignity. What authority endorses the person who makes nothing of what is essential to me?

Now, rather than abiding by a strict separation, compulsory in theory, untenable in practice, and rather than preferring an autonomy unbound from everything, at the risk of consulting with nothingness, it comes down to conceiving of autonomy as bounded. It is not incompatible with the call to a form of transcendence, the affirmation of a sort of revelation, and still less with the confession of a merciful God. The Creator made man in His image and in His likeness – which is to say, granting him the faculties of reason and of freedom, which is to say giving him the capability of living both free *and* bound, and therefore of religion.

History mutates, and the feasible error is to consider one stage of mutation as final. It is established today as never before that there is neither need nor legitimacy in using God whether to frame thinking, to base, or to certify it. But more than ever, there is a duty to think together so that God may come into the idea. The secular approach to truth also has its theomorphic side, and employs the absolute in its own way, when, as Pope Emeritus Benedict XVI has observed, it is an absolute of relativisms. Rationality does not equate to Pure Reason. Convictions and motivations do not correspond to a logic expressible in equations. The refusal to share them publicly, explicitly and by name obliges humanity to live in two mutually airtight worlds: the world of reasons, free from all concrete and subjective experience of perplexity, and the world of affects, foreign to any reflexive and critical retort of certainty. This would leave the door wide open to the two fundamentalist temptations that loom over the future: rationalist reduction and religious excess.

France presents a singular case. She offered the world the gift of the separation of church and state, which in fact liberates the proclamation of the Kingdom from the thrones, principalities and dominions. It nonetheless remains the country where people struggle to understand that, while the religious and political orders are required to be kept distinct, no individual can be split between their private and their public side. A bizarre brand of anthropology governs the fantastic notion that faith might have its own private closet. But above all, it entails an incongruity: to reduce the religious solely to its subjective inwardness amounts to granting to politics the power to determine what is and what is not religious. That means breaching the freedom of conscience, and encroaching on the core of the person.

Political power does not, under democracy, have the right to infringe the rule of law that counts as its yardstick of truth. It is totalitarianism, on the contrary, that leads somebody to lie to themself so as to lie about themself. Such is the weakness of those who lay claim to be masters, as Aimé Césaire would say, and whose sole justification is brute force. Now democratic authorities have no jurisdiction over convictions, except when their violent and exclusive utterance comes to transgress public order. Past that point lies an abusive power liable to provoke precisely what it is their duty to prevent, namely the instrumentalization of the religious for identitarian motives, to the detriment of people's right to belief, of the common good, and of the truth that sets you free.

Yesterday, to run the risk of secularization entailed releasing humankind from superstition. Today it also means releasing God from prejudice, whatever its source. In France, as elsewhere, Christians, and Catholics among them, have to highlight to all of the careworn their historical experience of a secularity that is positive as long as it does not reinvent itself as a substitute religion. Here, for the Preachers, is something of a mission statement.

Freeing one another

God is no more dead than He is absent or elusive. Today it is humankind that no longer has a ready trust in those – whether people or institutions – who make mention of Him. In order to restore it, it is necessary to take the risk of conversation among thinking human creatures. The sole unforgivable surrender would be to judge impossible the communion of people, whereas it is implied in the very essence of Creation. If the Church came to view itself as a contingent of crack troops deployed to bear individual witness to a faith practised individually, the damage this would cause would do harm, not to the existence of God, but to the proclaiming of the Gospel.

It is through conversation, a word that echoes the beautiful and just affirmation of Blessed Paul VI in his encyclical *Ecclesiam Suam*, that the ecclesial body is built. What does the Church think of bioethics? But does the Church not contain men and women who are biologists, physicians, geneticists, obstetricians, and specialists in antenatal diagnosis or foetal medicine, just as it also contains ordinary men and women who must discern, in the light of their own experience of life and faith, how or how not to resort to the diverse possibilities offered by biomedicine? All these people exist and are believers. They belong to the Church. They also constitute the Church. It builds itself with them. It is itself in listening to them, walking in their company. Otherwise, the Church that speaks, that discerns, that declares would be nothing but a voiceless, or conversely too loquacious, abstraction. But the Church is not the Church without God's people, without shared faith, without facing up in solidarity to uncertainties, contradictions, and sometimes aporias – without communion.

In order to do this, the Church must converse with every seeker after truth, and it can do so all the more serenely because it confesses that the Truth, for the Church, is a person. Hence its place, at the foot of

Christ's Cross, is neither to be yielded nor appropriated. Its attention belongs to every man and woman, and to the privilege of friendship owed to all. In that sense it sees the present time as perfect, for it represents this moment in history when no one can lay claim to imposing their convictions on anybody else without receiving those of others in return, without conversing with others. This time of ours takes trust for granted, in that from the outset it credits each person with their own authenticity. Nothing can infringe on the vitality of a humanity that, by the grace of God, is no more reduced to laying down principles than it is to passing them by.

In the face of uncertainties, it therefore makes sense for us to help one another to take the risk of thinking and acting in conscience. And if the separation of the temporal from the spiritual is one of the great fruits of our era, modernity must not, under the guise of freedoms continually updated, arrive at the point of seeking to colonize the heartland of the person. The Gospel holds, for its part, that this inner conscience is not for colonizing, and that nor may it be, whether in the religious or in the political sphere.

However, a more surreptitious colonization of minds is going on. In the realm of the psyche at least, the digital world tends to override the more immediate notions of time and space that square with our finite condition. Human beings are vulnerable in the face of the unknown, and here they are invited, or compelled, to look for reassurance by dissolving themselves into an immaterial and infinite universe where it seems that nothing and no one will be able to remain unknown. What then is to become of the uncertainty and disquiet that make them human, when they can wear themselves out in plugging the holes in their inner being and the gaps in their knowledge by subjecting themselves to machine systems that know and think for and on behalf of them? In these days of plans and promises for artificial intelligence – impressive and threatening in equal measure – would it be inopportune not to draw comparisons between human greatness and the breadth of its Promethean mastery? Does this greatness not consist instead in the mutual vigilance that assures that each person dwells in peace through lives of autonomy and dependence, knowns and unknowns, virtue and weaknesses, solitude and attachments? To be sure, such a vigil has to beware of the paternalist pitfall: one never does know better than the other what is good for them. But the illusion of an utterly limitless autonomy opens the way to all sorts of hidden and nameless dependencies, where only a limited autonomy can make the person humble and courageous, free and in concord.

Here we see Merleau-Ponty's classic image: can a bird take flight without a branch to support it? One of the missions of the Order is indeed to keep such a watch over men and women that they may embark on the venture of their own freedom, and that its enacting should offer the chance to welcome the Good News of which they are the recipients and not the author. That means that it is not for Preachers to wave around a catalogue of truths. That is not their task. Each one must remain, both in the proper and in the figurative sense, a humble deliverer. For the dispatch to arrive at its destination, the Preacher sees to it that no veil should intervene to shut out the arrival of the truth as it displays itself in intellectual research, artistic creation and the hush of contemplation. That it does not get varnished over, made subservient, tailored to our own measure.

The jeopardy of the present-day world arises for many from the construction of artificial identities that isolate one person from another in order to sort them out into consumer categories, the better to instrumentalize them into sections of opinion, and to assign them to communities of ideology. If the Preacher wants to announce the truth that is Christ, he must wholeheartedly promote the freedom in which every human being is created, for that is their inalienable dignity.

Resolving the catastrophe

In the Gospel, when the leper, the blind or the lame ask Him to heal them, Jesus, drawing on Jewish tradition, announces that He will restore them by, reintegrating them in the heart of the Chosen People. Of this work of 'reweaving of life', Brother Roger of Taizé used to say that it can best be achieved through the credence granted to the younger generations, bearers of hope in the future. In this way he was pointing to the utter priority of today: only trust in the power of life gives the courage to disarm violence.

To reweave, to repair, or again to re-establish the assurance that humankind is one and the same: there is not one continent where the question of reconciliation does not arise in the sharpest of forms, be it in Bogotá, Bangui, Rangoon, Kiev, Seoul, Paris or Kinshasa. It is always a joy for me to see our brothers and sisters spending their lives responding to this need. What more do they bring to this task than do the international organizations dedicated to it? Their contemplation of the friendship of God with humankind. Does that seem flimsy? There is no good that counts for little. Our brothers and sisters are responding to the calls to have done with the regime of death, at this point of recoil from which hope may surface through the witness of the life-bringing Cross.

We can cultivate our sense of goodness and charity, foster justice for all, fight for every person's dignity. But to reweave our humanity from within, in this deep chasm where it lies wounded – this we

cannot do with solely our own resources. The tailor
knows that, who when the fabric is too torn turns
it over, sorts out the weft, picks up the threads, and
reconstructs it from below to restore the material.
That is just what God does on Easter Day. On the
Cross, God in our midst makes manifest that He feels
the absurdity of our inhuman condition, confronts it,
upturns and reverses it. The sole retort to inhumanity
lies in the blood and tears that stream from His own
humanity.

How are we going to live together, in the recollection
of the violence and betrayals, with the memory
of images of horror? How, if not by relying on the
conviction that He, the Living One, conquered death,
that He descended into hell, and that He delivered the
human from death into life? This questioning and this
certainty, both of them terrible to experience, I have
encountered in places of unendurable tragedy, and
especially among young people who faced up to them
in the faith, and who made me say, with them, that
Salvation is real. It is at the outermost frontier of the
evil that they are liable to commit, that humankind
have it in them to outdo themselves, and acknowledge
themselves in every other human being, among them
the lost – determined not to abandon them to the Evil
one. This is why God wished to uphold humanity
through His Son – not one part of it against the other,

but as a whole. In order to somehow reweave what has 'frayed'.

Where and how can we say together, in unison, that we are human? Out of this common humanity, what do we want to receive, what do we have to offer? Can we do it without the promise of eschatological communion? Outside the perspective of the Kingdom, achievements stay only in human sight, perfections on the human scale that make the human an eternal Sisyphus. They do not count for nothing, but nor do they save anything, in so far as they patch up the fabric ready for the next tear. The communities we clumsily construct, and the words of peace that we murmur, are as so many doors opened by the promise held in the renewal of the world at the end of time.

This is the practice of hope. We have no idea of the concrete shape of the ultimate state of which we see 'only reflections in a mirror' until the day when 'I shall know just as fully as I am myself known' (1 Cor. 13: 12). But the sacrament is like an icon of the Kingdom that is coming. When the Church defines itself as the body of Christ, sign of the promised communion, of the Covenant, the sacrament of salvation, it expresses it through the Eucharist. For there to be sacrament, there has to be a concrete, solid substance. In this case, this substance is the prayerful community. Its offertory is the torn tunic, the underside of the world.

At mass, the greeting precedes the liturgy of the Word, and the liturgy of the Word precedes the liturgy of the offertory. When faced with the tragic and the unspeakable, it is better to be silent and to listen hard to the human words that attempt, by naming the inhuman as found in everyday experience, to disarm violence, to leave behind the labyrinth of sorrow, to disalienate memories from their suffering, to break down the killing walls of silence. The retelling of the catastrophe enables all those involved, including those who gave up humanity, who killed or tortured, to be mentioned and summoned together again as human beings. The Word forms the first act of forgiveness that Vladimir Jankélévitch, a witness of the Nazi horror, counted as what gives a man, above all else, the capacity to live, again and anew, as a man. It is this, the Word, that puts us in contact with the underside of the world.

Tirelessly to seek out the path on which people grow aware through the Word – whereas barbarism, exploitation, injustice and indifference risk instilling the delusion that they are mere objects – amounts to admitting that the Church is pervaded by what pervades humankind, that it cannot go unscathed by the crises undergone by humankind; that it is hurt by what hurts humankind; that its life is as complex as is humankind's, and this for the same – and strictly human – reasons. The hope that it harbours with respect to the economics of salvation is that conversion is always possible, upheld by the strength and loving kindness of mercy. Nevertheless, the power of consolation that it contains is one that surpasses resignation.

Some brothers and sisters have been or still are brought smack up against such disasters, and are never the same ever after. In these appalling situations they also confront their own humanity, that no less appalling perplexity before the evil that one human can do to another. To gamble on kindness, hope and peace is certainly magnificent and true. But when evil seems everywhere triumphant, and to be shattering all things, there hovers the essential question: where is my God? Most often, one among the worst afflicted will bring the reply: He is here, with us, in the midst of us, hanging from the Cross.

Consolation does not come about without the consolidation of this humanity, wounded and bound for glory. In this, it is quasi-'sacramental', eucharistic. Love works mysteriously in adversity. Even in the fall appears the path to liberation. When the child falls, and is inconsolable, discouraged, bitter and ashamed, the father holds him tight to soothe him in a gesture of protection. The Celestial Father himself is never disappointed seeing that his children, once consoled, jump out of his arms to frolic about again.

Our brothers and sisters posted to the underside of the world receive a hundredfold not what they give, but what they lose. Even in hell, they let their hand be taken by Him who descends into it and goes through it with us. He comes to seek them out, them and all of the others, so that they may be one. With Him and through Him, they know that humankind is beautiful, for it is able to withstand him who would have us believe – and this is the Divider – that it cannot love.

Finding mercy

God tells us: 'Take the world, increase it, be its gardeners.' Does He not know who we are? And yet still he trusts us – just as Jesus, asleep in the bottom of a boat as the storm raged over Lake Tiberias, trusted those at the helm (Luke 8: 22–5). Each time we tell the Christ that it is too late, that we are too much at fault or too worn out, each time, untiringly, He repeats that we can be born anew if we so wish. The Church has the task of voicing this trust, of proclaiming this nearness, and it tells itself this both in the nearness and in the trust that God alone can bestow on it. This was summed up splendidly in the remark of our brother Thomas Aquinas: 'Now it is most fitting that he who associates with others should conform to their manner of living' (*Summa Theologica* IIIa, Q. 40, Art. 3).[11]

With God, trust has ever to be ventured in the knowledge that it can be refused, since the founding act of Christianity relies upon the trusting coming among us of God's Son – not before thrice announcing that He will be rejected. All the same, He comes and He is here. Neither an institution of slogans nor a factory of rites made to measure, the Church must show itself for what it is, a 'Samaritan' communion. We do not comprise a limited company, organized in hierarchy; we are the people of God, of whom God declares that it is the people of His daughters and His sons. This Church–People, mystery of the body of Christ, is no longer a sum of individuals. In the course of human history, the Church–communion is the sacrament of the ultimate mystery that will see 'God with his people' (Rev. 21: 3).

The eschatological – because sacramental – dimension that makes up the Church also concerns the concrete life of all the communities that live within the Church, and therefore too the religious communities. Domestic churches, regular households, they answer in their own way to the imperative of communion

---

[11] Translation from New Advent (http://www.newadvent.org/summa/4040.htm).

that founds the economics of salvation. Without community there is no true mercy, or rather mercy would be solely individual, and at risk of the arbitrary. Now mercy does not happen to just one person, in order for their errors to be forgiven, and their wounds dressed, but also, in so doing, to rebuild the Covenant of justice and peace, the nearness of God, for each and everyone. It is Advent.

In this sense, the encounter is sacramental to the extent that it proves authentic, driving out the doubt that one or other of those facing each other should seek to disown their word. One has to be present in order to become a presence. This process, following the Eucharist, continues to depend upon Him who offered Himself like no other. The sacred is not the sole preserve of the ritual space. Neither is it the be all and end all. Sanctity surpasses it. And it is God who sanctifies. The lot of the 'useless servant', which is to 'eat and drink' after the Master (Luke 17: 5–10), lies with the hunger and thirst for His light. The glory of mercy extends to those men and women who humbly strive to propagate it. Who experience the approach of the God of sanctity, that experience of which Henri-Dominique Lacordaire said that it consists in 'a kind of deification, which, without confusing the finite with the infinite, the created with the uncreated, places them in so close a relationship that not only does the human think like God, but God is in the human through a penetration of their substance, just as the fire is in the iron that it transfigures through its light and its heat without denaturing it or denaturing itself'.[12]

It is to serve the mystery of this 'nearness of God' that the Order is so much called upon to stride across borders and to build bridges. Its task of care is twofold, with a view both to human freedom and to the human capacity for communion, which it pursues in the conviction that the Covenant suffers no hard and fast limitation. The Order's task is to keep alive this desire never to cease to enlarge the tent of the Covenant, not so as to make up numbers, but because the Covenant accomplished by Jesus knows no limits – as illustrated by the mosaic above the doors of the basilica of Santa Sabina. For there is no limit to the merciful salvation of which the Church of Christ is called to be the sacrament.

Knowing the truth

Such is our faith, in the eager waiting to see the fullness of time achieved. When and how? Only He knows. But once again, Saint Dominic's experience guides us, he who arrived at a moment when havoc reigned both in the Church and in the world. The

---

[12] Translation by the translator of this text.

choice was between restoring discipline and setting out to preach the Gospel. Dominic did not falter. Proclaiming the Good News means opting for what is most rickety, most fragile and most contingent in humankind. It is making a clear choice for the breath of grace over the illusion of the law. Now the breath, in the Gospel, is called love, and it is the Spirit that 'makes all things new' (Isa. 65: 17; 2 Peter 3: 13; Rev. 21: 1).

Dominic claims no dominion over the truth. On the contrary he repudiates the dualist temptation to which such a pretension invariably leads, and which quickly comes to border on the specious. For him, the preaching of the mystery of the Incarnation is the way to open dialogue with the entropy that causes people and communities to close ranks so as to spare themselves any doctrinal doubt, moral discomfort or contradictory debate. Instead of which, he sends us off to preach the selfsame mystery of the Incarnation – and the praying of the Rosary opens this path. It is in the footsteps of God become man that we become Christians.

This mystery is established once and for always. The assurances that we derive from it could lead us to forget that the coming of the Son of God into our midst saves humankind precisely because He takes upon Himself each human, and all that is human, in order to transfigure all humanity into His likeness. And yet concerning this, as we survey our lives, is there no ground for doubt? Meditating on Christ's agony at Gethsemane, Maximus the Confessor, that Father among Fathers, shows that if Jesus had not doubted in His human flesh, He would not have completely redeemed us. The Cross itself stands up against systematic certainties and definitive solutions. Against them, it puts up the Christ in person.

To understand this, we must turn towards Mary, the Mother of God, who is also for us 'the Mother of Preachers'. Her place in the Order is central, for she is its prototype, its model, its reason and way of being. It is she, the first contemplative of the mystery, who shows the way towards the coming of mercy. All through the centuries, the prayer and preaching of the Rosary have made up the life of brothers and sisters all over the world, guiding their meditation on the life of Christ so that they may learn, following Mary's example, to 'treasure all these things and ponder them in her heart' (Luke 2: 19). Here, in the fullness of contemplation, runs the surest path to releasing a surge of evangelizing.

Dominic founded an Order, but he left no writings, any more than he passed on a watchword, even though the Preachers see themselves in the one word 'Truth'. Dominic reached a decision, though against any form of polarization. No, that is not a choice. There is no need to choose between mercy and justice, just as there is no need to choose between truth and mercy. As a result, the debates around what *Veritas* means for the Dominicans remain open. Here again Saint Thomas Aquinas comes to our aid with his *Commentary on the Gospel of St John*.

The Son, addressing the Father and speaking of those with whom He had entrusted Him, says: 'I kept those . . . true to your name' (John 17: 12). This statement is also a request, and this prayer is basic for the Preachers' life. It voices two realities inherent in the order of communion, one concerning the relation of the Son to the Father, the other concerning the relation between the Son and those whose Redeemer He is. This prayer places us at the heart of the divine dialogue, at the heart of the mystery of the Trinity, and therefore at the heart of the mission of the Son. It likewise places us in a moment of intercession. Which, for the Order, proves vital on two counts. On the one hand, preaching is rooted in the awareness that Salvation commands solidarity with all. On the other hand, the first commitment of a friar is to pray for all those men and women to whom he is sent to preach. From God to us and back again, the unity of communion outreaches all desire to reduce the truth to a simple rationality.

The Son prays to the Father. In speaking to Him, He speaks of Himself, who is to be glorified, and asks the Father to open before those He tends to a comparable destiny: 'Consecrate them in the truth', not without adding, in pledge of our humility: 'Your word is truth' (John 17: 14–18). In other words, even if it is true that those men and women that the Father entrusts to the Son may seek to make a rational formulation of the mystery summed up in Their exchange, it is the Divine Word that is truth. And that Word, is He, Jesus Christ. Thus, for the Order, to have 'Truth' as a watchword signifies that the model of the Preacher is Jesus, and Jesus the preacher, manifesting the truth of the Father.

Because of this, the brothers and sisters are like the guardians of the perpetual inadequacy of human reason. At the crossroads between philosophy, science and theology, in magnificent pages concerning the hope of intelligibility, the philosopher Jean Ladrière shows how much more important is the desire for truth than its always inchoate formulation, and turns to recalling the eschatological structure of reason, always open to a future that it cannot itself contain.

So there is no truth to blaze abroad. What is proclaimed is the Name of Jesus Christ, and in that case, yes, it announces the truth. The genius of Dominic is to have grasped that study is indeed an essential observance, because it enables us to discover that eschatological shortfall of reason, and to cultivate the desire for it. Our relation to truth is thus one of vigil. It keeps alive the memory that the refusal to see humankind take hostage the divine, stamping the seal of eternity on a truth made to its measure, behaving like owners of the sacred and the holy, drove Jesus to His Passion. Our work of humility towards truth must invite us to meditate on truth humiliated. Christ accepted being cast out by all in order to reveal that the truth that unites Him with the Father cannot be commandeered.

With Him, the question is to be as authentic as I can be in my relation with myself, with others and with God. This vigilance, in which heart and reason stand mutual guard over each other, calls for resisting all absolutization of truths that most often prove sequential – strings of reasoning – as instanced more and more in the field of science. Now, if theology is a science, its practice entails the same process. To do less means reducing the space that belongs to God, as required by the revelation of His truth, through which He wants to consecrate us, in which He wishes to have us take part – that horizon of eschatological hope which already allows us to communicate with Him.

However, what Dominic realized is that our very reason helps us to avoid such a reduction, so little true intelligence is there with no authentic heart. Face to face with the tragic, in lives that border on the absurd, it is crystal clear that He alone, the Christ, was able to confront the abyss without getting lost there and stumbling upon the Leviathan. He alone, cross-questioned in the truth of His person, on behalf of the power of lies, although He was the Truth, but jeered at, humiliated, tortured, put to death. He alone could look evil directly in the eye. He could travel the length and breadth of emptiness and live.

EPILOGUE

As I conclude this book, which, finally, I have more let slip than deliberately written, what more is there to say? Except that, with every mention of the condition of 'Dominican' throughout these pages, the simple word 'Christian' would suffice. A commitment in a religious fraternity amounts to renewing the promises of baptism.

Eight centuries after Dominic, the grace is bestowed on the Preachers of taking part in the confirmation of the Order. So as to continue, in unity, to proclaim the Gospel of Christ. Not without having, once again, entrusted our mission, our personal lives and our membership of Preachers' communities to the mercy of God. Is all to be resumed and recommenced? Without a doubt. Our vocation is at stake. And that is to say, our joy.

Such is our life. When we make our profession, the rite is of the simplest. Following the reading of the Gospel, the friar prostrates himself while the prior says: 'What do you seek?' The friar answers: 'God's mercy and yours.' The prior says: 'Arise.' Following the homily, the brother places his hands in the prior's, and with their hands resting on the Book of

Constitutions, he commits himself until death: 'Go and preach!'

Only the Father's mercy makes our tradition possible. Only the Incarnation of the Word spreads mercy in abundance. Only the Holy Spirit changes the coming of mercy into working memory. That is what the Order goes out to preach. It is for that reason that the Order affirms preaching as a path of holiness in the conversion to the preached Word. In the midst of the Dominican iconography, so flourishing over the span of time and place, one of Dominic's points of reference remained the Baptist and Precursor: 'He who comes. He must grow greater, I must grow less.' (John 3: 30). That, I believe, is the best that could happen to a Preacher.

As a friar, in the footsteps of Dominic, I have professed unto death – that is, until that moment when He will say to me: 'Are you going on?' That question will mark the entry into a dynamic of prayer, study, and unbroken proclamation of the truth contemplated at last in its entirety. Into the joy of a growing fraternity and an enduring knowledge. At that instant again, at that tipping point into what we call eternity, evangelization will reign supreme: proclamation of the Name. The Word will have the last say of all.

Rome, Whitsun 2018